What's
the
Big
Deal?
about sex
Loving
God's Way

Cover and inside design by Dina Sorn
Edited by Dale Reeves and Leslie Durden

Library of Congress Cataloging-in-Publication Data:
Burgen, Jim, 1962-
    What's the big deal about sex : loving God's way / by Jim Burgen.
        p.   cm.
    Includes bibliographical references.
    ISBN 0-7847-1099-6
    1. Sex--Religious aspects--Christianity.   2. Sexual ethics for teenagers.
    I. Title.
    BT708.B88   1999
    241'.66--dc21
                                                                99-24219
                                                                CIP

The Standard Publishing Company, Cincinnati, Ohio.
A division of Standex International Corporation.

What's the Big Deal?

about sex

Loving God's Way

Jim Burgen

EMPOWERED™ Youth Products
Standard Publishing
Cincinnati, Ohio

contents

Getting Started

1

chapter one
Getting Started

OK, I've never written a book before. But I've read a lot of books. Does that count? I wish I could tell you that I am a great student who loves to dive into a deep book and discover the plot or the deep, philosophical message. But honestly, if it doesn't have pictures, I don't last long. I don't like reading about theories or hypothetical situations. I'm looking for stories and lessons I can identify with. My favorite part of a book is when I can say, "Yeah, I've been there before" or "I've felt like that too."

If you get bored with this book, stick it in a drawer and forget about it. But, I hope that you won't be bored. The goal of this book is to help you make good decisions about your life. One thing we all know is true: This life is full of hard choices and decisions.

Some people are asking the question, "What's the big deal about sex?" They might be thinking, "All of my friends are 'doing it.'" The *big deal* is that God really cares about you and has an awesome plan for your life, but figuring out that plan and following it are tough . . . especially when it comes to love and romance. This book is as real as I can make it. It's practical. It's relevant. It's real. It's about goals. It's about making plans. It's about success. It's about failure. It's about forgiveness—lots of forgiveness. I hope it helps.

All right, let's start with some easy questions:
1. Have you ever wanted to go on a date?
2. Do you ever see yourself falling in love and getting married?

3. Someday, do you want to have sex? (I told you this book was going to be real.)

Dating, love, marriage and sex—hopefully in that order. That's the plan anyway. And that's what this book is about. I recently polled some high school students and asked, "Do you want to get married? Why?" The responses were very interesting.

The majority of girls answered similarly, "Yes, I want to feel loved and I want to have a family to take care of." Most of the guys wanted to be married as well, but their reasons were slightly different: "Yes, I don't want to be alone; I want to share my life and be with someone."

The reasons may be different, but most people see dating, love, marriage and a sexual relationship in their future.

Let's back up for a minute. How did this whole man/woman, sex, dating, marriage thing get started? The best place to begin is where everything got started—the Bible. Genesis 1 gives us an overview of how men and women came into existence. This is *what* happened.

Genesis 1:26, 27 states, *"Then God said, 'Let us make man* [the word translates "mankind" or "humans"] *in our image, in our likeness, and let them rule over the fish of the sea and the birds of the air, over the livestock, over all the earth, and over all the creatures that move along the ground.' So God created man in his own image, in the image of God he created him; male and female he created them."*

That's what happened. Genesis 2 tells us *how* it happened.

"*The* LORD *God formed the man* [this time the word translates "the male man"—not the mailman, male as in "guys"] *from the dust of the ground and breathed into his nostrils the breath of life, and the man became a living being* [or soul]" *(Genesis 2:7).*

Quick review: God made the man (male) first, and the man was alone in the garden with the animals. Let's read on:

"*The* LORD *God said, 'It is not good for the man* [male] *to be alone. I will make a helper suitable for him.'* ["Suitable for him" means "that fits him."] *Now the* LORD *God had formed out of the ground all the beasts of the field and all the birds of the air. He brought them to the man to see what he would name them; and whatever the man called each living creature, that was its name. So the man gave names to all the livestock, the birds of the air and all the beasts of the field. But for Adam no suitable helper was found* [that fit him]. *So the* LORD *God caused the man to fall into a deep sleep; and while he was sleeping, he took one of the man's ribs and closed up the place with flesh. Then the* LORD *God made a woman from the rib he had taken out of the man, and he brought her to the man" (Genesis 2:18-22).*

Now, I can't give you the exact details, but can you imagine Adam when he woke up and saw this naked woman sitting there? "Hello. . . . Wow!"

Imagine waking up tomorrow morning, and there, on the end

of your bed is a naked person of the opposite sex. "What are you doing here?" you ask.

"God made me especially for you."

(gulp) "For me? Uhhhh, Mom, I won't be going to school today."

Again, what is my purpose in writing this book on love, sex, dating and marriage? I am convinced that God has a perfect timetable and a plan for each of us. But we always try to get ahead of God and make our own plans. And we always mess up or, at best, don't enjoy life as God intended us to. His plan is perfect. I really like what Elisabeth Elliot, one of my favorite authors, said: "I wish everyone could practice the 'Adam method' of relationships. Simply sleep (rest) in the Lord, and at the right time, He will bring you what you need." What a great plan!

I casually dated different girls through high school and my first year of college. Robin, my wife, dated one guy all through high school. They even talked about getting married, but it didn't work out.

Then she went to college and one day in the cafeteria, on an innocent trip to the salad bar, she looked up from the lettuce and—WOW, there I was—all tanned from a summer of life-guarding. (I was really good at spinning my whistle around my finger.) Right then she knew, "I'm going to marry him." (She even called her mom and told her she had just met the man she was going to marry.)

We were both on our college swim team. I practiced hard and really desired to be competitive. Robin was in it purely for the recreational and entertainment value. One night in practice, she jumped into my lane. I stopped and stood up to see who had messed up my lap. There, standing in front of me was a skinny, dripping-wet answer to prayer.

She asked me if I wanted to play "sea otter," a water game that she had invented where you swim around without using your arms. I didn't want to, but soon, we were laughing and splashing around. Before long, we encountered one of the dangers of swimming: weird, funky things hanging out of your nose. We both screamed and dove under the water . . . and a great relationship began (three years of dating and 14 years and counting of marriage).

Somehow I knew this relationship would be special. It was right. And from the time I started dating Robin, I knew God approved. Now, I didn't love her—yet, but I knew that God had plans for this relationship.

I am convinced that if you will be patient and wait on God, who has a plan for your life, he will work it out for you. Let me repeat: If you will wait on God, he will bring you everything you need. His plan includes all areas of your life, including your romantic life—especially your sex life.

God may choose to call you to a life of singleness, so that you can be fully devoted to him (see 1 Corinthians 7:1, 32-35). If that is the case, God will give you a peace about that calling.

Some of his greatest servants were single. And God's own Son, Jesus Christ, was single.

God's plan is better than anything you could rush out and find yourself. The purpose of this book is to teach you how and why to wait for God, and what to be looking for as he reveals and brings his plan to you.

Naked and Unashamed

Let's look at the Bible again:

> "The man said, 'This is now bone of my bones and flesh of my flesh; she shall be called "woman," for she was taken out of man.' For this reason a man will leave his father and mother and be united to his wife, and they will become one flesh. The man and his wife were both naked, and they felt no shame" (Genesis 2:23-25).

Isn't "naked" a funny word? In Kentucky, we pronounce it "nekk-id." That's even better. Go ahead, say it. Doesn't it make you giggle?

Little kids love to be "nekk-id." When my son, Jordan, was two or three years old, it was everything we could do to keep clothes on him. After bath time, forget it. He would slip out of the bathroom, grab his plastic guitar, jump into the middle of the living room sofa and the concert began.

Little kids love it. But the older we get, the more paranoid we

feel. We wouldn't be caught dead in public naked. (Wait a
minute, I guess that's good!) We get private, locking our d⟨
and closing our curtains. Even when we're alone and nake
we feel weird. But, then we get married and—WHOOPEE .
we're nekk-id and unashamed!

Let's see, where were we? Oh yeah—God's plan. What I wa⟩
to do is look at God's plan for your romantic relationships. I
think that you are going to find out some things that will rea
ly help you as you work out your love life.

Now, maybe you've read one chapter of this book and you
have already said to yourself that what I am about to say is
old-fashioned. It's not cool. This is the twenty-first century,
after all. Lighten up!

I'll make a deal with you. If you are satisfied with what
today's society is saying about sex and relationships (in spite
of the AIDS epidemic, rampant divorces, millions of abortio⟩
and Hollywood's shallowness), if you are satisfied with wha
out there and that's what you want for yourself, then throw
this book away. Don't read another word. But, if you want
more for your life, then you are gonna love this.

Grab a Bible or read along in this book. We'll refer to the I
often because that's the best place to start. If you do use ⟩
own Bible, feel free to underline it or write in the margin
OK. I don't think God will care and you'll always have it
you. Ready? Here we go.

Getting Personal

1. *Do you want to get married? Why?*

2. *How does it make you feel to hear that God has a plan for your life, including your romantic life?*

3. *Do you think God's plan is a better plan than you could come up with?*

4. *Do you think that God's plan will make you happy?*

5. *Are you willing to trust God's plan?*

6. *Think back to the "Adam method" mentioned earlier. Do you believe that if you will "rest in the Lord," God will bring you what you need in the right time?*

7. *Make a list of words that describe dating, love, marriage and sex as seen from a present-day point of view. How do Hollywood movies, popular music, television or magazines present "normal" romantic relationships? Does this list of words describe what you want for your own romantic relationship?*

8. *What are some words that might describe what God wants for your romantic relationship?*

Equal . . .
But Different

2

Equal . . . But Different

Quick review: We've looked at what God created (mankind). We've looked at how God created them (male and female). But to fully realize how God's plan is going to work, we must take a closer look at the male/female thing. The Declaration of Independence declares that "all men (mankind) are created equal." That's true. That's biblical. But being equal does not mean everyone is identical.

Listen to what 1 Peter 3:7 says:

"Husbands, in the same way be considerate [understanding] *as you live with your wives, and treat them with respect* [honor them] *as the weaker partner and as heirs* [sisters] *with you of the gracious gift of life, so that nothing will hinder your prayers."*

Picture it like this: God is at the top corner of the triangle; men and women are at the lower two corners of the triangle. Although a man and a woman are on an equal level, each has a unique corner of the triangle to fill. (The really cool thing is that as the man and woman move closer towards God, they also move closer to each other—more on that later.)

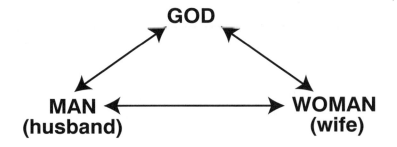

Now, think about what you just read in 1 Peter: Husband, wife—partners; same level, but different. That's what we are going to talk about. Men and women are different. Duh!

First Peter gives a message to men as husbands or boyfriends. Here it is: "You need to be considerate. You need to understand the differences." Differences? What do you mean? Guys, you need to treat women with honor and respect. Why? Because the biggest difference is that they (the women) are the weaker partner. (Hold on, feminist, don't blow a gasket!) "Weaker" actually means "more delicate, more precious of the two of you: handle with care." Equal in value to God (same level of the triangle), but more precious in care.

It's like when you have company and your mom brings out the good dishes. Maybe they are carefully wrapped up and stored in a box and are brought out only for special occasions. On normal days, you might use the everyday dishes. They get banged around, slammed in the dishwasher, left in the sink. But on special occasions, it's time for the good stuff, the delicate stuff, the expensive stuff. And your mom warns you over and over again, "Be careful!" Why? Because they are of great value.

Listen and be impressed by my grasp of the Hebrew language. Actually, I don't speak or understand Hebrew, but this is one thing that I actually remember from a sermon I heard a long time ago. It's really cool. The Hebrew word for "man" is *ish*; it means "hard." The Hebrew word for woman is *ish sha*; it means "soft."

See? Men and women are different. As different as hard and soft. "Thanks, Jim! You are so deep. That's really helpful. NOT!" No really, listen. They're more different than you might think. I'll show you.

1. Men and women are physically different.

Duh! OK, there's the obvious: the sex organ, breast thing, but there are a lot of other differences too. This is so cool.

Have you noticed that the fashion trend has been for girls to wear guys' baggy jeans for a "unisex" look? But, girls, remember the first time you tried to pull up a pair of guys' jeans like you pull up your own jeans? They went up only so far, then they stopped. Why? Because they were made for a guy. The manufacturer knew that a man's skeleton is different from a woman's. Girls have longer hips in order to have babies.

Guys, I wouldn't recommend this, but if you were to try on girls' jeans the waist would hit you about the armpits. (You probably would want to lock your door. This could be hard to explain, "Uh, I was just comparing my body to a girl's body.") Wait—there are more physical differences!

Girls are bigger inside. They have larger stomachs (sorry, girls), kidneys, liver and appendix. But they have smaller lungs, meaning they have less endurance. This is a general rule. I know girls who can run circles around guys, but from a genetic, across-the-board representation, this is true.

And guys and girls are chemically different. If a girl has too many male hormones, she might grow a mustache or she might have a "masculine" figure. Have you ever seen a female athlete on steroids? She begins to develop big shoulders and a deep voice. Many times, older women or those who for some reason lose their ability to produce female hormones experience a deepening of their voices and increased facial hair. What's the problem? The female hormones aren't balancing out the male hormones anymore.

Here's another difference that married men understand very well. Women can tolerate heat better and cold less than men. Just wait, guys. Someday, when you get married, you'll climb into bed and expect to see your wife in one of those sexy nighties. Nope. Flannel gown, long johns, socks—not real sexy, but very warm.

Men and women are even different in their blood composition. Females contain more water in their blood and fewer red cells (hemoglobin). This blood difference can account for why many women tire more easily and have less stamina than many men. Guys, next time you're running around and she gets tired, you'll understand.

Here's another difference. Many girls faint more often than most guys. Why? Girls have a more active thyroid. This also explains why they cry more readily and show more emotion. Now, if a guy exhibits typical female characteristics such as a high voice, tiring easily, fainting or crying, he is labeled a "sissy" or a "homosexual." That's not fair and it certainly is not right, but these are characteristics we associate with the female sex.

2. Men and women are emotionally different.

Ladies, you need to know that men have two huge fears:
1. The fear of being dominated;
2. The fear of being found inadequate, not measuring up.

If they feel either of these is true, their egos are shattered. Guys, women have one basic need that overshadows all others. What is it? The need to feel loved. If a girl feels like a guy loves her, there isn't too much that she won't do or give to him. The big problem, though, is that many girls want love so much, they give away too much in order to get it. I have counseled many girls who consented to have sex with their boyfriends because they were afraid that they would "lose his love" if they didn't. Afterward, they see the mistake that they made, but when the need to feel love is there, many young ladies will trade everything to feel it. We'll talk more about this in chapters seven and eight.

Again, 1 Peter 3:7 reminds us, "Guys, you need to be understanding of this." Men, I'll be honest with you. There is nothing harder for a man than to try to understand a woman. Just when you think you do, it changes. And, although I can't

speak from personal experience, I've been told that men are
equally baffling to women.

Robin and I used to have big fights in college. We'd sit by a
fountain at Milligan College, arguing. Robin would yell and I'd
pout. And right in the middle, she'd ask, "Can you even tell
me what we're fighting about?" "Uhhh . . . Nope." She'd
remind me why we were fighting and go back to yelling. Later,
she'd ask again if I remembered. "Nope." She'd start crying
and I'd start apologizing. (If you have dated for any length of
time, you know exactly what I'm talking about.)

Guys, how many of you have ever felt frustrated and totally
lost when a female—she doesn't even have to be your girlfriend—is crying? We don't have a clue. Sure, it's because we
are different—and, sometimes, not too bright in the sensitivity
department.

Think back to our triangle. Men and women are on an equal
plane; neither is closer to God or more favored by him—but
each is different. God says, "Men, recognize this difference."
You have the responsibility to treat a woman with respect and
sensitivity and to grant her honor. How? By being a man to
her. How? By taking care of her and protecting her. When you
are dating, it can start by carrying things for her, opening the
door, helping her. Girls, let him honor you. You're worth it. It
doesn't mean you are weak; it means you are precious. Any
guy worth dating, let alone marrying, ought to recognize this.

The emotional needs of men and women can be very different.

Genesis 2:18 says, "'It is not good for the man to be alone.'" Marriage is designed to address the problem of loneliness. Man was alone and he was lonely. So, God created woman.

Most men need a woman in their lives. It's true. Many men cannot survive nearly as well without marriage as they can being married. On the other hand, women do much better alone than men do. For example, if a couple has been married for a while, and the wife dies, if the man does not remarry, very often he will die earlier than if he remarries. Why? He's lonely.

But if the husband dies, a woman is like the rabbit advertising batteries: she just keeps on going. Check out the local nursing home. Women far outnumber men. Think back to the poll asking, "Why do you want to get married?" What does a man need? Someone to share his life with. He doesn't want to be alone.

These needs can sometimes lead to problems. For instance, if a man comes from a bad home life, or his parents are divorced, or his house was a place of turmoil and unhappiness, he may go looking for a woman who can fulfill the things that he feels he missed out on. Many guys marry a "second mother." Any marriage counselor will tell you that this is not healthy, but it is some men's answer to being alone.

Girls, on the other hand, are more of a "herd animal." If they get lonely, they just get together with the girls. Girls do everything in herds. Every time I go to a restaurant with a bunch of students involved in my ministry, some girl will stand up and ask, "Who needs to go?" About five girls will jump up and head off to the bathroom. (I wonder what would happen if a guy stood up and asked, "Who needs to go?" I'm sure that it would involve beatings and bloodshed.) A guy likes his male friends, but he wants a girlfriend.

Here's another danger: A girl may feel sorry for a guy, date him, take care of him, rescue and mother him. A girl sees a lonely guy or a guy going through some problems and, because of her tender, caretaking nature determines, "He needs me. I'll marry him and fix him" (big mistake, which becomes a big counseling topic).

3. Men and women are mentally different.

One of the biggest revolutions in the study of the brain is the growing acknowledgment that there *are* physical differences between men's and women's brains. For instance, one difference is a structure called SDN (or sexually dimorphic nucleus), a cluster of cells in the hypothalamus that's $2\frac{1}{2}$ times bigger in males than in females. The hypothalamus is the region of the brain that serves as a regulator of hunger, thirst, sleep, sexuality and emotions. In laboratory rats, the SDN plays a role in mating and territorial behavior, though its function in humans remains unknown.[1]

Without getting too technical, another difference is in the way the left and right hemispheres in a woman's brain are connected by means of something similar to a computer cable, whereas a man's right and left sides of his brain are not as integrated. Some researchers suspect that this closer connection might explain "women's intuition."[2] Guys, that's why your girlfriend suspects someone's motives long before you have a clue, and why she is more often right about people than you are.

On average, men's brains are 15 percent larger than women's, which doesn't mean a lot except that guys have much bigger heads (in more ways than one!). Why do men have a much harder time asking for directions? Because men, in general, create "mental maps" and think they can find their way on their own. Women tend to remember physical objects, or land-marks, and will find their way based on correct information.

Another difference is in the way men and women process their emotions. Generally, women seem to be more skilled than men in expressing their emotions, because of the differ-ent ways they "think" about them. This also means that a woman is more prone to experiencing anxiety, depression, irrational fears or panic disorders than a man. Because of his need to be "in control," a man may be more likely to experi-ence abusive anger than a woman.

What does all this mean? Neither the male nor the female brain is superior—they're just different. If we are open to learning from one another, our individual strengths and weaknesses can provide balance. As you enter into a relationship with a mem-ber of the opposite sex, be aware of the different ways the other person thinks. Educating yourself about any potential dangers may save you some real trouble down the road.

4. Men and women are assigned different roles by God.

Here is the difference that may tick off some of you girls. According to the Bible, it is the man who is to be the *initiator* in a relationship, and the woman who is to be the responder. The man is to go after the girl, not the girl after the guy. Genesis 2:24 says it is the man who leaves (his family) and unites with his wife. (The Hebrew word *dabaq* means to cleave, pursue hard, to catch by pursuit.)

I know: this is the twenty-first century and females have taken over male roles. The woman is the aggressor. She sends the notes. She makes the phone calls. She may even ask the guy out. Men will respond, but this role reversal is unhealthy because it gives the man the upper hand. Ladies, you may get dates, but you have set yourself up for the man to be in power and to take from you what he wants, and then move on. You need to realize that when you are being pursued, you have total control of the situation. You don't realize the power that you have in one little word: "NO!"

You see, you think that guys just decide to ask you out on a whim. No way! A lot of pain goes into the process. Remember one of the male fears, the fear of being found to be inadequate? A guy agonizes, "What if she says no? What if she rejects me? What if she laughs in my face?"

So, guys practice in front of the mirror. We rehearse asking you out on a date. We get tongue-tied. We go over our speech a million times, check our breath and put on extra deodorant. We finally work up the nerve and . . . ask. (Even if we appear cool and confident, we are shaking in our boots.)

Some girls are just downright mean with their responses. "Go out with you? Oh, thanks, I'd rather have my entire body waxed." Some women try to be nice, but don't succeed. One time in college, a guy asked Robin out and she actually responded, "Thanks, but I have to clean out my purse that night." That's cold!

Women hold the power of the response. When the girl answers yes, the guy may appear "cool," but when he gets home, he jumps around the room singing into the mirror, holding his hairbrush like a microphone. When the girl says no, as soon as she is out of sight, the guy looks for the nearest cliff to throw himself off.

According to the Bible, the male is the pursuer, the initiator. Women were made to be with men. This is not a sexist statement. A wife's primary role is to live for her husband as a helper, a counterpart, a "completer," not a "competer." This relationship ideal may not be politically correct or popular. However, the goal of this book is not to copy the world but to identify and follow God's plan the way he set it up. In God's plan, the man is the initiator.

Ladies, you are different. From the day of conception, you behaved differently. If you take tiny infants and leave them alone, the boys will be drawn to trucks and bats and noise; the girls will be drawn to dolls and dress-up and conversation (not exclusively, but as a general rule).

We're different. Picture it like this. A man and woman are like two pieces of a puzzle. Where one piece of the puzzle is cut out, the other piece fits in. Where the man is strong, the woman is weak. Where the man is weak, the woman is strong. The goal is not to duplicate each other; duplication leads to conflict. The goal is to dovetail, to complement, to fit together—to become one flesh, one whole.

We're different, and the difference is good. One role is not better. It's just different. Celebrate and live within that difference.

Some men and women have a very special and unique calling: the call to remain single. In Matthew 19:12, Jesus talked about those who remain single and celibate because they believe that they can serve the kingdom better in this state. Paul, in 1 Corinthians 7:1-9, even encourages those who can to remain single for the sake of kingdom work. He is not forbidding people to marry; he is just commenting that, for many, Christian service is so encompassing that time for a quality relationship might be a problem.

The goal of marriage is to complement the other person, to provide companionship and support for the other person. This in no way implies that if you aren't in a relationship or married, you are an incomplete person. Philippians 4:19 assures that "my God will meet all your needs according to his glorious riches in Christ Jesus." When you are a Christian, the presence of Christ in your life makes you a whole person. Until you have a personal relationship with Christ, you are not fully prepared to live life, whether single or married.

I love being a man. And I love women—one in particular. I don't want to rule her and I don't want her to rule me. I want to take care of her and share my life with her. What do you want for yourself?

Something in this chapter may have rubbed you the wrong way. In the next few chapters, we are going to look at the differences and roles of men and women. If something bothers you, keep reading because we are just getting started. The next chapter is about sex. You might want to turn on the air conditioner: it could get very warm in here.

Getting Personal

1. *How does it make you feel when you read in 1 Peter 3:7 that the wife is the "weaker" partner (remember, "weaker" translates "more delicate")?*

2. *What are some ways that a man should "respect" or "honor" a woman in light of the differences you just read about?*

3. *Guys have two huge fears: the fear of being found inadequate (not measuring up) and the fear of being dominated by a girl. Guys, take a minute to consider some areas in your life where you manifest these fears. (Be honest!)*

4. What does a guy risk when he asks a girl to go out on a date?

5. Girls, one of your greatest needs is to feel loved. What are some ways that you would know that a guy truly loved you?

6. You read that if a woman pursues a man, she has set herself up to be used (or even abused). Why would this be the case?

Safe
Sex?

3

Safe Sex?

Let's review what we've already covered. God created man but it wasn't good for him to be alone. So, God created woman to be man's partner, to help and complement him.

We talked about the differences between these two creations. Men and women are different:
1. physically, in their "plumbing" and a whole lot more
2. emotionally, in the man's need to feel adequate versus the woman's need to feel loved
3. mentally, in their thinking processes and chemical make-up of the brain
4. relationally, in which men are to be the initiators and women are to be the responders

We started with a simple question: "Do you see yourself dating, falling in love, marrying and being involved in a sexual relationship?"

The next question is, "If you do, what *kind* of a relationship do you want?" If you agree with what Hollywood, rock stars and pop culture define as love, good luck. However, very few of us want that kind of love. We want something far better.

Recently, I had the privilege of participating in an open forum, a debate where I presented my views and a woman who had a Ph.D. in Sexual Deviancy and Marriage and Family argued the opposite position. (How would you explain to your mom that you were majoring in sexual deviancy?) The assigned question we were to address was, "Are we failing our youth in terms of sex education?"

Safe Sex?

The doctor presented her viewpoint first. Her answer could be summed up as: "Yes, we are failing our children. We need more education and more accessible contraceptives (condoms, pills and abortion). Teenagers are going to have sex. It's unrealistic to expect anything less. There is no way to stop them. We need to prevent pregnancy and keep sex 'safe.'"

This argument always puzzles me. Ask your medical doctor if he or she believes in "safe sex." Follow that question with, "If your own son or daughter were going to have sex with someone you knew was HIV positive, would the presence of a condom set your mind at ease?" Watch the doctor stutter around with an answer.

My answer was, "No, we're not failing them. They are living up to society's expectations for them. We have told them, 'Hey, we give up. You have sexual urges. Fulfill them. OK, it would probably be better if you waited, but we know you won't. So here is a condom—protect yourself.'"

I think our government agrees more with the Ph.D.'s premise, having spent billions of dollars on contraceptives and "safe sex" programs as opposed to a few million dollars on abstinence programs. Why? Because that's what the news media, MTV and Hollywood say our kids want to hear and what they need. But is it, really?

In a recent poll, nearly 9 out of 10 high school students questioned said they didn't want condoms handed out in their school or in the vicinity of their school. In another national poll, when questioned about the number one issue that needs to be addressed with teenagers, 99% responded, "How do I say no to sexual pressure?" They listed this issue above drugs, alcohol, violence, suicide, pregnancy and pornography.[1]

Sure, many kids are having sex. Some studies estimate that two-thirds to three-quarters of all graduating seniors have had at least one sexual encounter. A more recent survey suggests that fewer than 25% have actually "gone all the way." It depends on who you ask and who is being honest. However, almost all young people are saying, "We want to be able to say no; help us know how to say no. Give us a better reason to wait than to give in."

That's the biggest question that has to be answered: Why? Why wait for marriage? Why be monogamous (staying with one partner for life)? Why not have sex now? Let's look at some possible answers!

1. Because you might die!

Believe it or not, this is not a good enough answer. Fear is not an effective deterrent. Let's look at the facts: First of all, condoms fail one out of six times—not great odds. (Even the condom package states that a condom is no guarantee against disease.) The AIDS virus is so small, it is able to pass through the microscopic holes in a latex condom. "Safe sex" or "smart sex" is a joke! If you'll notice, the media now call it *safer* sex."

Safe Sex?

Secondly, most guys don't wear a condom regularly.[2] Many guys I have talked to have promised to "try to remember." If two people are going at it hot and heavy, and someone says, "Sorry, I didn't bring a condom," rarely will both agree to call it quits. They're probably not going to just say, "Hey, let's go bowling instead."

In the next few years, over 100 million people will be HIV positive or will have already died. Some estimate that at the present time, one in 75 guys and one in 200 girls are already infected and don't even know it. One new HIV infection occurs each 54 seconds; one death from AIDS occurs each 9 minutes; 267 new AIDS cases are reported each day.[3]

AIDS has been the sixth leading cause of death among 15-24 year olds since 1991.[4] At the present time, if you contract AIDS, you are as good as dead. There is no cure. Worse, you may not even be aware that you are a carrier for 10 years or more. By that time, most will be married, possibly with children; and, if you are a carrier, all of your family members could be infected.

I recently met a man who had become a Christian 10 years ago. Since giving his life to Christ, he had been completely sexually abstinent. He is a talented songwriter and musician. We regularly sing worship choruses in our church that he has written. A few weeks ago, he was diagnosed with full-blown AIDS. His sexual activity before he became a Christian has caught up with him. God will always forgive sin, but the consequences of choices we made years ago may haunt us for the rest of our lives . . . and may even end them.

But you know what? Fear of death is not enough to force you to be abstinent.

2. OK, how about, because you might get pregnant?

Again, not a good enough reason. Every day 2,700 teens become pregnant. Every 24 hours, another 3,000 become sexually active and lose their virginity.[5] Some people might say, "It's OK, I'm on the pill." Sorry, not a good answer! The pill is not totally effective in older women, let alone with a teenage girl who hasn't established a regular menstrual cycle.

More than one million teenage girls become pregnant each year. Of that one million, just over three in ten choose to abort the baby. In 1994, that added up to 298,000 teen abortions for one year. As a country, the U.S. has topped 4,000 abortions a day. One-third of your generation has already been aborted.[6]

I don't think that anything you read here or see on TV or hear from a sermon will ever "scare" you into not having sex in the long term. Maybe it would work for a week or two. I could tell you a sad story of a life devastated by AIDS or show you a picture of an abortion and you would respond, "Gross!" and determine that that life wasn't for you. But your fear-inspired response would eventually fade. Why?

    1. Because very few people (especially teenagers) think that they are going to die anytime soon.

2. Very few teenage girls think that they could really get pregnant. That happens to "other people." Nearly every teenage couple who has found themselves in this situation and come to me for help has always said the same thing, "We never thought this would happen to us."

The sexual drive is very strong. Faced with sexual temptation, you can rationalize away your fears and override common sense. I am convinced that no one can "scare" you into not having sex.

Well then, what's the answer? Why shouldn't you have sex before marriage? I believe that this is a big question and to answer it, we have to go to a higher level. Higher than Top 40 music, the newest MTV vj, blockbuster Hollywood movie or U.S. Surgeon General.

Let's ask God. He created sex. What does he think about it?

Getting Personal

1. *Answer the question I debated with the Ph.D.: "Are we failing today's youth in terms of sex education?" Is the answer more easy access to contraceptives? Is the answer counseling on "how and why to say no"? What do you think?*

2. *What are some of the dangers in engaging in sex before marriage? What are some immediate dangers? What are some long-term dangers?*

3. Why aren't these reasons sufficient to keep people from engaging in sex before marriage?

4. Before you read the next chapter, make a list of some good reasons to wait until marriage for sexual activity.

Why Wait?

4

Why Wait?

OK, if you can't be "scared" into sexual abstinence before marriage, what is the answer? Let's look again to God's Word. In 1 Corinthians 6, a guy named Paul is writing to a group of people coming out of a really rough background. Corinth, the city where they lived, was comparable to New York City and Los Angeles rolled into one. The Corinthian church was full of people who used to commit adultery (cheat on their husbands/wives, sleep with their boy/girlfriends), who used to be homosexuals, drunks and thieves. The key words here are "used to be." You see, they had become Christians and God had changed them. Read along:

> "'Everything is permissible for me'—but not everything is beneficial. 'Everything is permissible for me'—but I will not be mastered by anything. 'Food is for the stomach and the stomach for food'—but God will destroy them both. The body is not meant for sexual immorality, but for the Lord, and the Lord for the body. By his power God raised the Lord from the dead, and he will raise us also. Do you not know that your bodies are members of Christ himself? Shall I then take the members of Christ and unite them with a prostitute? Never! Do you not know that he who unites himself with a prostitute is one with her in body? For it is said, 'The two will become one flesh.' But he who unites himself with the Lord is one with him in spirit" (1 Corinthians 6:12-17).

What does all of this mean? Paul writes, "You have the *ability* to do just about everything, but not everything is best for you."

I bet that Paul felt like your high school English teacher. He gave this great talk, this awesome lesson, and the "class" just sat there and stared at him with a blank stare like, "Huh . . . what are you talking about?" So Paul gives some examples. He explains, "It's like food. The stomach was created for food and food for the stomach. They have a natural relationship. They go together. But, if food becomes your master, you are going to suffer for it. Is food bad? No. Is the stomach wrong? No. They were meant to go together."

Then Paul turns to sex. "It's the same way with sex." Paul acknowledges that you have the ability (and the equipment) to do certain things. Once you hit puberty, you have hormones racing through your body. Things are growing on your body. Things are changing. You are on an emotional roller coaster. Your body is saying, "OK, upstairs, we're ready down here. Let's go!"

Here's a weird thought: Wouldn't it have been easier if God had made us like big Barbie and Ken dolls? Have you ever seen a naked Barbie or Ken doll? They have no parts. When it was time to get married, we could go down to some office to pick up our marriage license and then stop by the doctor to pick up our sex drives and equipment. "We'll take a marriage license and one of those and throw in a couple of those. Oh, no thanks, we'll wear them home."

But that's not what happens. Once you start developing sexually, the natural thing is to have sexual drives and desires. Paul says, you now have those abilities, but now is not the best time to use them. Why?

48

Well, let me give you my corny answers first. I've heard sex compared to a river. In its banks, it can power huge cities, provide food and transportation. But if it leaves its banks and floods, it kills and destroys. Are rivers bad? No, not if they are in their proper place.

I've heard sex compared to fire. Fire can keep you warm, cook your food and purify what's unclean. But it can also burn down your house and char your flesh. Is fire bad? Not when kept in the proper boundaries.

Paul is saying, "Leave it in the place where it needs to be." Sex, as beautiful as it was intended, can be devastating if it crosses its boundaries. Harmony Monahan, columnist, reports that according to the Department of Justice, one in three girls and one out of seven boys will be sexually molested before the age of 18; a woman is raped every 46 seconds in our country. Many convicted molesters, such as Ted Bundy, have confessed that they were acting out what they had viewed on TV or videos or seen depicted in pornographic magazines.

Why is there so much sexual abuse? Because the abuser fed an appetite that was created by what he or she had consumed visually, needing more with each exposure to get a sufficient level of excitement.

Now, I am not accusing you of being a sexual molester, but think about this: Remember the first time you held someone hand? You were nervous and your palms were sweaty. The next time the two of you were together, you grabbed the ha

and kept going. Remember the first time you put your arm around that special someone? You were nervous, but you went for it and were relieved when it was accepted. The next time, you barely hesitated before putting your arm around her. Remember that first kiss? You thought about it all night . . . then went for it or accepted it. Now, you kiss without a second thought. It's just natural. (If you're an experienced dater, you know exactly what I'm talking about; if you're not, you'll have to trust the voice of experience.)

The progression just keeps on going. There's the next time . . . and the next time . . . and eventually, you are sitting in the back seat of a car barely dressed asking, "What's next?" What's *left* to do? (Duh!)

Are our bodies bad? No! Is sex evil? No! Our bodies are striving, even aching, for that for which they were designed. But as much as they are suited (and desire) to have sex, it's not time. Or as Paul puts it, "It's not in your best interest; it's not profitable." This is not what God had in mind for you. The body was not meant for this. Well, what *was* it meant for? (That's the $10,000.00 question!)

1. Your body was meant for your spouse.

Remember how God set it up in the Garden of Eden? A man and woman were to become "one flesh," which involves a physical, psychological and spiritual joining. If that's not enough to con-

vince you to wait, here is the main, the ultimate, the best reason to wait on God's plan for sex:

2. Your body was meant for the Lord!

Your body was created to be used by the Lord for the things he has in mind, to be joined to him. It's not even *your* body; it belongs to God. He made it, paid for it and lives in it.

> *"Do you not know that your body is a temple of the Holy Spirit, who is in you, whom you have received from God? You are not your own; you were bought at a price. Therefore honor God with your body"* (1 Corinthians 6:19, 20).

Question: So what happens if you become "one flesh," joined with someone other than your spouse? Answer: You drag your future spouse (the one for whom it was meant) into it as well! On a physical level, the AIDS epidemic has brought this principle clearly into focus. When you have sex with anyone, you are having sex with that person, and any other person that they might have had sex with, and so on. That's the physical reality.

But I want to tell you that there is an even deeper level—a spiritual level—of violation that has also occurred. When you have sex with someone other than the one God has in mind for you, you drag that person into your future relationship with your spouse. Let me explain:

A few years ago, a movie entitled *The Last Temptation of Christ* came out. In this film, Jesus is depicted having sex with a woman. When this film was released, many Christians were outraged. How dare anyone portray Jesus as doing such an immoral thing! Think about it, how would you feel if I took a pornographic movie or magazine and glued the face of Jesus on some of the characters so that he appeared to be "participating" in the pornographic act? You'd be offended. You would tell me that it was sick, blasphemous, terrible. How different is it when we, especially we who claim to be followers of Christ and have him living inside of us, join ourselves to sex partners who are not our spouses? We have literally done the same thing.

One night after church, a young man approached me and exclaimed, "I don't understand the big deal about this sex stuff. I mean, all animals have sexual urges. It's just a physical act."

Yeah, right! Let's say that you walk outside and there in your driveway is your cat having sex with another cat. You just kind of roll your eyes and shake your head. But the next day, you see your cat up in a tree having sex with a different cat. What would you think? I doubt that you'd run after your cat yelling, "Bad cat, sleazy cat, cheap, slutty cat!" You'd probably just laugh and say, "Cats will be cats." You expect it. That's what cats do.

Now, let's say that you and your significant other have just finished having sex. Your partner leans over to you and whispers in your ear, "That was really fun. Tomorrow, I am going to do that with someone else." How would you feel? That it was just a physical act? I don't think so.

In the movie *Indecent Proposal*, a millionaire gives a million dollars to a couple as payment for one night with the wife of the other man. Even though both husband and wife agreed to the proposition, saying it was "just sex," the marriage begins to fall apart shortly after that night. The bulk of the movie is spent working through the results of the "deal." In the end, the money is thrown away and the couple begins a long, difficult process of healing.

Just a physical act? It is more than the joining of two bodies into one sex act. It is the culmination of intimacy that God designed for marriage as an ultimate sharing. God created it for marriage and blesses it there. Anyplace else, he calls it wrong and off limits. He calls it sin! When you have sex before marriage, you are cheating your future mate and you are committing adultery against God.

Why wait to have sex until marriage? Because you have a higher purpose. Because you were made exclusively for one other person on this earth. Because your body was made for God's use. He made it. He purchased it with his blood. He lives in it, he's in charge and he says, "Wait!"

hy Wait?

etting Personal

Getting Personal

1. What does Paul mean when he says, "'Everything is permissible' . . . but not everything is beneficial" as it applies to sexual activity?

2. How does sexual activity create an "appetite" which "grows"?

3. Your body was meant for two things. What (or who) are they?

4. What is the problem with becoming "one flesh" at the wrong time?

5. Why wait to have sex until marriage?

How Can I Wait?

5

How Can I Wait?

Well, the next question is, How? How do I say no? How do I stay pure? I have all of these feelings, these desires, and my body and everything around me wants to go for it. How in the world can I wait, maybe for years, for sex? What if I *never* get to experience it?

Several years ago, my children came to me and asked me to teach them to ride a bicycle. We started with the basics. "These are the pedals: they go round and round. This is how you keep your balance. This is how you turn. These are the brakes." Eventually, they became familiar with how the machinery worked and the laws of gravity and locomotion.

But I also included several safety features in our lessons. I provided them with helmets. I fastened training wheels to the back of each bike. Now, why would I do that? Is it because I didn't trust them? No. Is it because I didn't have faith in them? No. I knew that eventually, they would be able to ride and have a great time riding their bikes. Why then? Because I love them, and until they had the power, strength and ability to ride with confidence, I wanted to protect them from as many painful situations as possible.

Eventually, the training wheels came off, but not until after they had learned some skills and coping mechanisms to deal with their new environment. Let me share some "safety features," some "coping mechanisms" to help you deal with your new environment (your sexuality).

1. Stay in "safe" territory!

I know that sexual references are unavoidable in today's culture. They are on magazine covers and billboards everywhere we look. We can't control that but we don't have to make it worse by putting ourselves in danger. Certain situations and places are an invitation to trouble. Alone at home with your boyfriend or girlfriend would top the list. (Did you know that most high school girls who find themselves pregnant became pregnant from a sexual encounter right in their own bedrooms or houses while her parents were away at work or out doing errands?) If you put any two teenagers in love in a "home alone" situation, even the best Christian kids in the world, you are asking for trouble. Remember, physically your body is saying, "Go for it—do it!" Putting yourself in an environment like an empty house or a parked car is like pouring gasoline on a fire that's ready and willing to burn.

The Bible instructs us:
- "Flee [run away] from sexual immorality" (1 Corinthians 6:18).
- "Flee the evil desires of youth [those situations which always seem to lead to trouble]" (2 Timothy 2:22).
- Jesus himself taught us to pray, "'Lead us not into temptation'" (Luke 11:4). The problem is Jesus won't lead us into tempting situations, but we frequently place ourselves in dangerous places.

Chapter Five

before you start walking!

2. Watch your step before you start walking!

What do I mean? If you are already in a sexual situation, most of the time it is too late to put on the brakes and say, "Hey, I think we've gone far enough!" The decision about how far to go needs to be made before the situation arises, long before you even decide to go on the date.

That means making some decisions and setting some limits *before* you ever become involved in a dating relationship. How far is far enough? I'm asked that question more than any other when it comes to the physical relationship between dating teens. But the real question being asked is "How far can I go before I'm considered bad by breaking the rules?" Usually, the person asking wants to go as close to the edge as possible before "crossing the line."

First of all, it's a bad question. The better questions are "How can I keep my relationship as pure as possible?" and "How close can I get to God and honor him in this relationship?" When you answer these questions, the "how far" question is answered as well (more on that later).

How close can I get to God? That's a great question. That's "riding the bike." But until you are at that point, let me give you a few "safety" suggestions. This is my "training wheels" version of "safe sex."

Can I Wait?

Don't let anything belonging to your body enter anything belonging to their body.

Is that clear enough? Let me explain further. This includes genital intercourse, but it also includes oral sex (using one partner's mouth as a substitute sex organ) or using your hands or fingers to touch and stimulate your partner's sex organs.

I'd even take it another step and include French kissing. No, I'm not kidding! Think about it: French kissing is an oral form of intercourse. When you French-kiss, your body is preparing to be "invaded" or entered by another person. Be honest: if you can French-kiss and not think about "doing it," you are a better person than I am. Simple rule . . . If it's yours, keep it out of theirs!

If it is covered by a one-piece bathing suit, leave it alone.

I like this guideline. If you respect this one, there is plenty left over to admire, but all within a relatively safe distance from danger. Think about it: there is still a lot left to do! You can hold hands, give good, safe hugs, put your arm around their shoulder or waist, even share a tender, gentle kiss. But because you know that there is a line that you won't cross, it frees you from the pressure of having to prove that you can.

Here's the final suggestion for keeping yourself pure:

3. The only way that you can say no on the outside is if you have Christ living on the inside.

Chapter Five

If you don't have a relationship with Jesus Christ, then why not have sex? Why not go along with the world and its set of values and standards? But if you do have Christ living in you, then you have chosen a better standard, a higher purpose and a much purer objective.

Listen, I realize that staying pure in this day and age is tough. And I know that by today's standards, what I just described to you may seem impossible to accomplish. Believe me, I understand. I remember when Robin and I were dating. Man, we had some close calls. Most of those close calls occurred when we abandoned the precautions I just described to you. If it weren't for God, we'd have really messed up. Even with God, it was incredibly tough.

I remember one time, one of Robin's college friends left town for the weekend and gave Robin the keys to her apartment. Robin fixed a cozy little dinner for me and we sat down on the couch to "watch a movie." Bad idea! Boom! We came to decision time.

Now, sometimes, I "wanted to" and Robin was strong. Sometimes Robin "wanted to" and I was strong. Now, we were in trouble. We both "wanted to." But for some reason (probably the Holy Spirit), I stood up and went into the bathroom. I closed (and locked) the door, looked in the mirror . . . and started crying. (I know, not very "macho.") Why?

Because on the other side of that door was a woman that I loved and wanted very much. I wanted to have sex with her—

I loved her and I knew that she loved and wanted me too. And in just a few months, we were going to be married. But I also knew that it wasn't right. A few minutes later, Robin knocked on the door. "Jim, are you all right?" "Yes," I cried . . . and for the next 30 minutes, we sat on opposite sides of a locked door and cried and talked. Why? Because we loved each other so much and we "wanted to," but we were called to a higher standard.

Remember when we read in 1 Corinthians 6 that all things are "permissible but not beneficial"? Verse 14 goes on to say that the same power that raised Christ from the dead has the power to raise you. It also has the power to change you and give you the strength to do the things you *need* to do and deep down *want* to do.

Now, let's answer one more big question: What if I've already made a mistake? What if I've already lost my virginity? What if I've already gone too far sexually? What if I've already "joined" myself with another person—or several people? What if I feel that this part of my life is out of control? What can I do?

Realize that God may hate what you did, but he loves you.

He is not shocked by it. As a matter of fact, he saw it happen. What you have done is exactly the reason his Son died on a cross 2,000 years ago—to pay for a sin that you hadn't even committed yet. He knew that one day you would need forgiveness. When you become a Christian, God erases your past. To him, it never happened. He has the ability to "forget." We'll talk more about his awesome love in chapter thirteen.

Do you remember when you were a little kid and you would play kick ball? You kicked the ball the best that you could, but it went in entirely the wrong direction. Maybe it took a bad bounce; maybe you misjudged it; maybe you just blew it. And you wish you could take it back. Remember what you would yell? "Do over!" With God, that is his specialty. With God, you get a "do-over," another chance.

Now, obviously, he is not going to re-create your virginity. There will be only one "first time." But he can re-create purity. He can remove guilt. And he does take away condemnation.

Determine from this point on that, with God's help, your body is off limits to everyone except your spouse after marriage—and to God.
 You are not your own. You were created for your spouse and you were paid for by God. Someday, you will stand before your husband or wife, and you will give yourself to them. What do you want to give them? You want to give them a pure and spotless gift. "It was tough. It was hard to protect. It was attacked from all sides. But from the day I gave myself to God, I saved myself for you." What a great gift!

etting Personal

Getting Personal

1. *Take a moment to answer these questions: "What do you want your marriage to 'look' like? What are the qualities and characteristics you would like to have present in your romantic relationships?"*

2. *If asked by a friend, how would you answer this question: "Why should I wait until I am married before I enter into a sexual relationship?"*

3. *Take out a separate piece of paper. Write down your standards or "safeguards" regarding a physical relationship with a date. This might include what you are looking for in a date, how far you will go physically and the locations where you plan to be alone with a date.*

4. *By refusing to cross certain lines in a physical relationship, are you denying that there is a sexual attraction between you and the other person? If the answer is no, then what are you doing?*

5. *How does God's "presence" in your life help you stay in line with his sexual guidelines?*

6. *If you've already made some sexual mistakes, what should you do now and from this point on?*

"I Love You"

6

"I Love You"

An all-too-common story:
She was in her early teens. She had always looked forward to these teenage years. They were supposed to be the best years of her life. That's what people said.

He was much older and was very popular at school. He was the kind of guy that everyone wanted to be around: talented, handsome, admired. For some reason, he liked her and soon they became boyfriend and girlfriend. One day, he said to her, "I love you."

She said nothing. She didn't love him. But she loved the popularity he gained for her and she was blinded by the attention everyone gave her when he was around. Everyone seemed to know her name.

He asked, "Can I express my love to you?" She said she wasn't ready. He said, "I love you." No reply. Later, he said that he had shown his love to someone else, yet he did not really love her. This was different. She said, "It's all right." But it wasn't.

He said, "I love you." She said nothing. So many friends! Everyone wanted to talk to her, even the other boys had started pursuing her. So, she stayed with him because he "loved" her. He told her again that he had shown his love to someone else, but repeated that he really didn't love that girl. He even pointed out the girl to her. "There she is, right over there."

She looked away. She felt threatened. He said, "I love you." She looked down and softly said, "I love you, too." He asked her to show him her love. She didn't want to but she didn't want to

67

I Love You"

lose him, so she showed him her love. He said, "Show me again!" She said, "No," and she ran away. She felt alone, violated, naive, used, so she broke up with him.

He said, "Take me back! I love you!" She rejected him. A few days later, he was in "love" with someone else. She felt impure, unwholesome, used, drowning in shame, guilty, afraid to love again or be loved. She couldn't change the past. She felt like it had stained her life and the stain wouldn't ever come out. She was young—very young. But she felt very old.

This story is all too common. This story is reality. It happens hundreds of times each week. Maybe you are one of the characters in the story. Here is an excerpt from one of many similar letters I have received:

> *Dear Jim,*
>
> *Premarital sex was the worst mistake I ever made. I had sex with someone I thought that I loved and that loved me. I really thought we would be together forever. I was wrong. I wish I could push a big "rewind" button and take it all back, but I can't.*
>
> *I know that God has forgiven me of my sin, but I hate that I will never again be a virgin. God has forgiven and forgotten, but I'm having a hard time forgiving myself and I know I'll never forget. Someday, I will give myself to my husband, but he won't be my first—although I'll wish that he was.*

Love! There is probably no more overused word in our society today than the word "love." We have one word, and it's supposed to mean a hundred different things. You can't turn on the radio for more than a few seconds without hearing a song about love. Years ago, songs proclaimed, "Love makes the world go 'round," and "What the world needs now is love, sweet love."

Our parents grew up with concepts like "love at first sight" and songs with words such as "Some enchanted evening, you will meet a stranger, you will look across a crowded room and your eyes will meet, and bells will ring, and you'll know." Then pop music brought its shallow lyrics onto the scene. Remember the Doors? They sang, "Hello, I love you, won't you tell me your name?" Now, there's a deep relationship!

One of the theme songs while I was in high school was Meatloaf's "Paradise by the Dashboard Lights." In this song, the boy plans to end up in a parked car. Step by step he plots to have sex with the girl. As in a baseball game, he gets to first base, then second, then third. Just as he is about to go for a "home run," she says, "Stop! Before we go any further, I need to hear those words: I love you."

So she sings, "Do you love me? Will you love me forever? Do you need me? Will you never leave me? Will you make me so happy for the rest of my life? Will you love me forever? Will you make me your wife? Do you love me?"

Finally, realizing that unless he says the magic words, he won't get what he wants, he promises his eternal "love" to her. The song ends with the boy praying for the end of time, because he can't stand the girl anymore, but he's stuck.

I Love You"

It makes a great song. It makes lousy reality. But too often, it *is* reality. Every year when I teach a series of lessons about sex and dating, I always get a letter or two: "Dear Jim, I wish I had heard that earlier—it's too late for me." (I get those letters from both guys and girls!)

I hate the phrase, "It's too late for me." First of all, in God's eyes, it is never too late. You've never done "too much" for him to forgive or heal. (I know I sound like a broken record, but I want to say it a thousand times: God is always wanting to forgive a person who comes to him for help.) But I also hate that phrase, "It's too late for me," because it is a desperate cry saying, "I went where I shouldn't have gone. I wish that it hadn't happened . . . if only I'd known."

What is "true love"? It's not what the world says about love, not what the latest song on the radio describes as love, but what the One who invented love defines love to be.

Someday, you will give someone your heart. You will look at them and say to them, "I love you." How will you know if you really do? What does that mean? Again, let's go back to the Bible. Ancient Greek literature mentions four kinds of love. The Bible mentions three of them.

1. *Storgé* **love** (pronounced stor-gay)

Storgé is natural, human love. For example, "I love America. I love my parents. I love mankind. I love horses. I love pizza. I love the idea. I would love to go to Hawaii." Storgé love is not mentioned in the Bible.

2. *Eros* love (pronounced air-oss)

Eros love is passionate love. We get our word *erotic* from this word. Eros love causes physical arousal. Eros love is what makes you get that pit in your stomach when your special someone walks into the room, or your arm brushes against them, or you touch for the first time. It is emotional arousal based on body or sexual chemistry. Eros love is concerned with "*my* happiness." (This is what you do for *me*. You make *me* feel this way.)

3. *Phileo* love (pronounced fill-eh-o)

Phileo love is an affectionate love. It is the love of liking: I like you. I like spending time with you. "I" and "you" have become "we." We are friends. We have fun together. Phileo is "what is called out of you by the qualities of another person." I see this in you, and I like it. I like you because of something you do or are. Phileo love could be summed up as "*our* happiness" (concern for relationship, being together, we get along).

4. *Agapé* love (pronounced uh-gop-ay)

Agapé love is unconditional love. It desires the other's highest good. What can I do for you? No matter what, your highest good is what I will pursue. Agapé love is not based on conditions. Agapé love is a "no matter what" love, which can be summarized as "*your* happiness." (Does it make *the other person* better?)

Think back to the opening story of this chapter. The guy felt eros love. He felt a strong physical attraction. The girl felt none. Yet she was willing to be involved sexually because she didn't want to lose his attention.

I Love You"

In a recent poll of teenagers I know who have been sexually active, 47% of guys and 65% of girls admitted that they had said yes to sex even though they didn't want to. Why?

The reasons varied:
1. I didn't want to hurt her feelings.
2. I didn't know how to say no.
3. I was afraid he would stop liking me.
4. I was afraid she would think I was inadequate—not a real man.
5. I felt pressured. After all, all of my friends are doing it, or so I thought.
6. Because we thought we loved one another. (I thought he loved me. I thought it would last forever. I thought that this person was "the one").

This seems like as good a time as any to have a special talk with just the girls (but guys, you need to read this and learn as well). Ladies, there is a popular perception that there is something wrong with you if you don't have a boyfriend (or with some people, if you aren't sexually active). Who made up that rule? I know of girls whose self-identity and self-esteem are totally wrapped up in whether they are currently "going out" or not. If they are "in a relationship" or being given male attention, everything is OK. They are complete. They feel safe.

But if there is no guy, no attention, no date, no phone calls, they panic. They feel like something is wrong with them. They believe that they need to change or do something to get some male attention or affection.

This places them in a very dangerous and vulnerable position. Think back to the opening story and song lyrics of this chapter. The girls in both situations were willing to trade their sexual purity for promises of love, security and attention. They were willing to pay a huge price for what they were sure would deliver intimacy and love. Listen carefully, ladies: *Sex will never buy you love!* Love will never be the result of sex. Sex, by God's design, is designed to be the result of love, never the cause. That's why it will work perfectly only in marriage.

I've met too many girls who thought that in order to have value they needed a guy in their life, and in order to catch and keep a guy in their life, they needed to provide him with sex. Everyone—*everyone*—I have met who tried to find value in the arms of another person has failed.

Girls (and guys, for that matter), there is one question you need to answer long before you ever go on the first date: Where do you find your value? Listen, you have value because God says you do. He loves you the way you are. God looks at you and thinks you are beautiful. Tall, skinny, short, stocky, athletic, clumsy, graceful, awkward—God really likes you. If God carried a wallet, he'd have your picture in it. Proud fathers love to show people pictures in their wallets. I think God walks around Heaven showing your picture to the angels: "Look, isn't she awesome? That's just the way I made her—perfect."

You are special because you are special to God. And if you never, ever had a date, that wouldn't change. As a matter of fact, until you can believe and accept this fact, you aren't ready to even

I Love You"

think about dating. If you are looking to another person to give you value, then you will never find it. Only God can fill that place in your heart.

You are special. Remember that. God says that your soul is worth dying for, and your body—your physical body—has such value that God calls it a "temple" and chooses to live in it. So he reminds and instructs you, "Hey, you have tremendous value . . . so much so that I died just to rescue you . . . now, honor me with your body" (1 Corinthians 6:19, 20). You have value. Things that have value don't get passed around like a football. Save your body, your lips, your hugs, your intimate words and secrets for the right time . . . and the right person.

In my whole life, I have told only one girl that I loved her—just one (not counting my mom which is a totally different kind of love). Why just one girl? Because it is a serious thing to say. I remember when Robin first told me that she loved me. It was on a bench in front of her dorm. I didn't know what to say. I had never said it and no girl had ever said it to me. I had to think. A few days later, I knew that I could say it and mean it: "Robin, I love you too." What did I mean by "I love you"? Simple. I am ready to agapé you.

Question: When should you say, "I love you"?
Answer: Not until you are ready to love with agapé love.

Let's look at the sequence of a love relationship. When do you say the magic words?

Most relationships begin with an eros/phileo type of love. You
see someone, you get nervous. "Wow, they're cute!" You have a
physical attraction. That's OK! Don't run away, but remain in
control. Eros love is important, but it is not "it" and it's certainly not the time to say, "I love you." Why? Because eros is not
enough. Why? Because of real life. Because we no longer live in
the Garden of Eden. Because circumstances change. Because we
have problems and conflicts. Because sex takes a few moments
and there are 23 other hours in the day to deal with. Because
sex and physical appearance change over the years, as does
their priority in your life.

Sexual, eros love is important. It is from God. He could have
said, "You want to have kids? Here are three easy steps: bam—
here's a baby." He could have made us like earthworms who
don't need a partner to have babies. (Boring!) But God made it
exciting. I love getting that pit in my stomach when Robin says
or does something (that I'm not going to tell you about). I like to
remember the last time I held her or think about the next time.
Sexual love is a gift from God. "Thanks, God!"

But eros is not enough to build a lasting relationship out of. If
you feel only eros for someone, but not phileo, don't date them.
They may be beautiful or handsome, but what if they have no
personality? What if you can't have a meaningful conversation?
I know lots of divorced couples who had a very active sex life
while they were married. They just couldn't get along outside of
the bedroom. What if, as beautiful as this individual is, he or
she treats you in a degrading manner? Ultimately you will have
to compromise something to continue the relationship.

I Love You"

On the other hand, phileo love (friendship, I see this in you, I like being with you), before eros is a much better alternative. Friendship is a great place to start a relationship. Let God add in the eros, the sexual attraction, at the right time.

Getting Personal

1. *Both girls in the opening stories were willing to have sex. What did they hope to gain?*

2. *If you are experiencing eros love, what does that mean?*

3. *If you feel phileo love, what kind of love is this?*

4. *How is agapé love different from eros or phileo?*

5. *If we are not to depend on other people as our primary source for value or esteem, where should we turn to find our definition of value?*

6. *Why is it dangerous to enter into any dating relationship before we answer the value question?*

Agapé Love

7

Agapé Love

OK, so, you feel eros, and you like being with your boyfriend. You can share your deepest thoughts with him; you can tell him anything. You really trust him (phileo). Are you ready? Should you tell him that you are in love with him? Is now the time? Not yet. When you think—correction: when you know—you are willing to agapé him, then it may be time. The other two (eros/phileo) are there, but they are joined by agapé.

How do you know if it's agapé? Let me give you a checklist of six things that you can do beginning right now in your relationships before you say the big words. "Do I love this person? Really? Let's see, I like to spend time with this special someone. We have fun. I definitely feel eros, but what about agapé?"

1. Agapé love is unconditional and it's forever!

In 1 Corinthians 13:7, 8, the apostle Paul says that agapé love bears all things and endures all things—it never fails (gives out).

Dating is fun, but it's not always realistic. Think about it. In dating, you see the other person at his or her best. Guys, you pick the girl up at the front door. She has on her nicest outfit. She's spent a week and a half on her hair. Girls, his hair is actually combed, he smells great, he holds the door open for you and he has a romantic evening all planned—dinner, flowers, walks in the moonlight.

But agapé love is for better and for worse. What does "worse" mean? Imagine the other person unlovely: bad breath, mad, moody. Imagine them making a wrong decision, acting hateful. What if one day down the road, they turn physically ugly—could you live with them long-term? Really?

What if they were sick, not with a 24-hour flu, but for a long time and they couldn't meet your needs? What if they couldn't have sex with you—ever? Would you love them still?

What if one day they tell you they don't love you anymore? Would you still be willing to stay with them?

See, it's not as easy and glamorous as it first seems. It's not just candlelight and roses. Agapé love is unconditional. Are you willing to love them and stay with them—*no matter what?* Not as long as they meet your needs or can give back to you. Not as long as they do their part. Not as long as they love you back. Agapé love *never* fails. It has no conditions. It is permanent. Now, you might think, "Well, I don't think that God would expect me to stay no matter what." Yes, he does: agapé is forever! Don't say it until you can do it.

2. Agapé love is active!

Agapé love is willing to demonstrate. It's easy to say the words, "I love you." It's hard to live them. Poetry, soft music and flowers are all easy symbols, but let me see your love by the way you live.

Again, 1 Corinthians 13:4-7 says that agapé love is kind and protects. How do I know you agapé me? Because you want to protect me. Protect? What do I mean? "I want you (sexually), but I will not touch you until we are married. Why? Because I seek your highest good. I want to make you better. I want to help you. I want to protect you from guilt, from becoming a parent too early, from pulling you away from your obedience to God. So, I will wait for you. I will serve you—even when it's inconvenient (or even frustrating) to me. I love you so much, I wouldn't do anything or allow anything to harm you—even my own needs or desires."

3. Agapé love is sacrificial.

It does not seek its own. It focuses on giving, not receiving. "'For God so *loved* the world that he *gave* his one and only Son'" (John 3:16). In Romans 5:8, Paul says that Christ demonstrated his love for us before we ever knew his name or loved him back. Before we had done anything to deserve it, he sacrificed his life for us.

In Ephesians 5:22-33, the apostle Paul compares what Christ has done for us, how he has loved us and provided for us, to the relationship that husbands and wives are to have for each other:

> *Wives, <u>submit</u> to your husbands as to the Lord. For the husband is the head of the wife as Christ is the head of the church, his body, of which he is the Savior. Now as the church <u>submits</u> to Christ, so also wives should <u>submit</u> to their husbands in everything.*
>
> *Husbands, love your wives, just as Christ loved the*

*church and <u>gave</u> <u>himself</u> <u>up</u> for her, to make her holy,
cleansing her by the <u>washing</u> with water through the word,
and to present her to himself as a radiant church, without
stain or wrinkle or any other blemish, but holy and blameless. In this same way, husbands <u>ought</u> to love their wives
as their own bodies. He who loves his wife loves himself.
After all, no one ever hated his own body, but he <u>feeds</u> <u>and</u>
<u>cares</u> for it, just as Christ does the church—for we are
members of his body. "For this reason a man will leave his
father and mother and be united to his wife, and the two
will become one flesh." This is a profound mystery—but I
am talking about Christ and the church. However, each
one of you also must <u>love</u> his wife as he loves himself, and
the wife must <u>respect</u> her husband.* (Emphasis mine.)

Look back at these verses. Notice how many words and phras-
es have to do with serving, with giving up rights, with personal sacrifice: *submit, gave himself up, washing, feeds* and *cares,
love, respect.* These aren't always fun words. They involve
humility. They involve service. They involve sacrifice.

Agapé love is sacrificial. I sacrifice my wants, my desires,
even my rights, for your good. I will serve you, even before I
know your name.

When a woman is pregnant, before she has ever held the baby,
before it even has a name, she takes vitamins, gives up certain
habits and eats special food for the good of her child. She has
decided that the payoff is worth the wait. Agapé loves says the
same thing. "I sacrifice my intense desire to have sex with you,

because I want what's best for you. I love my future husband or wife too much to give my body to someone else. Maybe that will be you and we will remember this moment and it will be one of our best memories. But I will also serve you by not taking, or even asking for, something that isn't mine."

4. Agapé love is a choice.

In John 13:34, Jesus commands us to love one another. If he can instruct us to do something, it must be possible to make a decision to do it. If it were involuntary, then it would be cruel to demand it.

Popular music and Hollywood have romanticized the concept of "falling in love." It's kind of like falling in a hole—"I can't help falling in love with you. I don't know when it happened. I couldn't help it, I couldn't control it—I just fell in love with you." The problem is that if you can "fall" into love, and it's not your fault, then you can "fall" out of love, and that's not your fault either.

Many parents have given their children the big "We're getting a divorce" talk. Usually, it includes, "We still love each other, but in a different way." What they're saying is, "We don't feel a certain way anymore."

Agapé love says, "I'm staying anyway, and I'll trust God to take care of the feeling part. I may struggle with phileo or eros for someone else. But I will still agapé you."

Agapé love never fails; it suffers through. It's unconditional, meaning there are no "but what ifs." It even includes staying faithful when the other person stops loving you back. It keeps going.

Wow, that's impossible! You're right. It is! If you haven't gotten the picture yet, let me be blunt: agapé love is hard work! I don't know how anyone could ever do it unless the love and power of God are living inside of them. I said in the first chapter, the best thing that a couple can have going for them is that they both love God.

I will be very honest with you, and I know my wife would say the same thing. There have been times in our marriage, when the only, the *only* thing that kept us going wasn't sex, wasn't the fun and laughter and meaningful conversations. It was the commitment that we had made to stick together, even through the ugly, sad, hurtful, depressed, unromantic times. These periods haven't always lasted just a few minutes of a day; sometimes they have involved days, weeks, months. Some conflicts and "for worses" have gone on for years. "Hey, I agapé you. I'm staying. I promised."

5. Agapé love is learned; it is not automatic.

It takes practice. You have to train yourself. How? Well, maybe, it starts with the people that you live with right now: parents, brothers and sisters, grandparents. Sometimes they are wrong; sometimes they make mistakes. But don't write them off. Work through the problem. No matter what it takes, don't quit.

Secondly, watch who you date and how the relationship starts and ends. Let me explain: Let's say you see someone that gives you feelings of eros, but they are in a relationship with someone else. Leave them alone. It is a "no win" situation. If you go after them, you have set a pattern for your life that declares, "No one is off limits." If they respond to you, they have sent out the message, "I'll stay with you, until something better comes along." (That's what they just did with the current relationship they dumped for you!) If you cheat on your boyfriend or girlfriend now, you'll probably carry that habit right on into your marriage with you. You've set a pattern: You are a cheater. (We'll spend the next chapter dealing with this entire area in more detail.)

That's why I think teenagers should be very cautious about long-term relationships in high school. They put pressure on you and put you in situations you shouldn't have to be in. I know that the expectation today is that everyone "should" have a boyfriend or girlfriend by a certain time. Who made up that rule? Listen, for the record, you have permission not to be in a serious relationship.

6. To love someone with agapé love, you must understand how much God loves you.

Agapé Love

He loves you no matter what you have done to yourself, to others or directly to him. He sees you at your best and at your worst. He even knows what mistakes you will make and what you will say and do to him in the future. Yet, knowing all of this about you, he was willing to allow his Son to die on a cross for you to provide a better way, to seek your good at his expense.

I greatly respect a few young ladies in my ministry who decided to forego dating for a year (and these girls were "very dateable," if you know what I mean). They made a commitment to spend an entire year focusing on their relationship with God before they took that step of entering the dating world. They understand that the best way to love their husbands later is to love God with all of their hearts now.

And, remember, God may call you to a life of singleness to be fully devoted to him, and him only. If he does, you'll know it. In the meantime, there's absolutely nothing wrong with "group dates," going out with several of your girl and guy friends to just have a good time together.

Love: it's a big thing. It's a special thing. Don't cheapen the words "I love you" with a definition that says, "You make me feel good. It's fun." Love is so much more.

Getting Personal

etting Personal

1. *What do we mean when we say, "Agapé love is for better and for worse"?*

2. *What's the difference between "talking" about love and "demonstrating" it?*

3. *How is agapé love sacrificial?*

4. *How can someone say that love is a "choice" and not an uncontrollable urge?*

5. *How can the habits you form now have an impact on your romantic relationships later?*

6. *What is the ultimate display of agapé love? Give examples of each of the first five characteristics as it applies to this display of agapé love.*

Divorce-Proof
Marriage

8

chapter eight
Divorce-Proof Marriage

This might seem like an odd time to insert a chapter on divorce. But based on the "forever" theme of the previous chapter, it is very appropriate. I'll be honest with you, in this chapter, you will find hard teachings, but if you will follow closely with an open mind and heart, you will see that everything I am about to say makes logical and biblical sense.

Let me explain what is *not* my goal. My purpose is not to bring condemnation on anyone or to point fingers at any person. My objective is to open the Bible and point the way toward a better life, the life that God has in mind for you. Please be honest with yourself and ask God to teach you his truth even if it's hard to hear.

We live in a strange world, a "disposable" world. For example, take a tour of the average bathroom. It's filled with disposable razors and throwaway cans, bottles and cartons. Use it up, throw it away and get another one. Commercials bombard us every day with advertisements that urge, "Dissatisfied? Try another brand. Switch to something else."

All over your house—disposable plates, cups, plastic forks, diapers, cameras, contact lenses. The list goes on and on. Or think about cars. Millions of people aren't buying cars anymore; they're leasing. Why? There is less risk. If you get bored with your car or a better model comes along, you can turn in the old one after two years with no penalties.

Disposability is everywhere. A few months ago, I took my family whale watching in San Diego. There was a huge sign that read, "Satisfaction guaranteed or you get your money back." If we don't see whales . . . if you don't like it . . . if it doesn't meet your expectations, we'll refund your money. No risks.

Everything is replaceable these days. Few people fix things anymore. They just get a new one. The defective or outdated one goes in the trash. Even the Bible acknowledges that most things are just temporary. Jesus warns against putting stock in possessions which rust and wear out and are destined for the city dump (Matthew 6:19).

In fact, there are really only a few things meant to last a lifetime. One is your eternal relationship with God. He says that once you enter into a relationship with him, it is eternal; it lasts forever. It has barely even begun until after you die.

But there is one other relationship here on earth that, once entered into, is for keeps, and that's marriage. As a matter of fact, in the Bible, marriage serves as a picture of how our relationship with Jesus is supposed to be. Jesus is the groom. We, the members of his church, are the bride, and the relationship is one of mutual love, protection, provision and care. We've already referred to this earlier, but let's review it one more time:

> *Wives, submit to your husbands as to the Lord. For the husband is the head of the wife as Christ is the head of the church, his body, of which he is the Savior. Now as the church submits to Christ, so also wives should submit to*

their husbands in everything.

Husbands, love your wives, just as Christ loved the church and gave himself up for her, to make her holy, cleansing her by the washing with water through the word, and to present her to himself as a radiant church, without stain or wrinkle or any other blemish, but holy and blameless. In this same way, husbands ought to love their wives as their own bodies. He who loves his wife loves himself. After all, no one ever hated his own body, but he feeds and cares for it, just as Christ does the church—for we are members of his body. "For this reason a man will leave his father and mother and be united to his wife, and the two will become one flesh." This is a profound mystery—but I am talking about Christ and the church. However, each one of you also must love his wife as he loves himself, and the wife must respect her husband (Ephesians 5:22-33).

Do you see the picture God gives us of marriage? Jesus (the groom) loves us (his bride), *protects* us, *provides* us with what we need (forgiveness and guidance) and cares for us. And we do the same for him—we love him by *providing* him with the worship and obedience he deserves and by *protecting* that relationship, keeping away from anything that might try to destroy it or separate us from him.

Question #1: If marriage is supposed to be a picture of our relationship with God, which lasts forever, and marriage is supposed to last forever, why has marriage become one of the most disposable items of our time?

I don't think I have to convince you that divorce is an epidemic in our country. The last I heard, around half of all marriages are now ending in divorce. Why? I think the answer is obvious if you'll stop and think. If Satan can minimize and destroy the importance of the picture, then he has a good chance of destroying the real thing.

Think about it: If Satan can get you to believe that marriage and divorce are no big deal, that when problems get too big or feelings ebb away the solution is just to abandon the whole relationship and find something else, then what's to stop you from assuming the same thing about God?

I think if a lot of us were honest, we would say we want to get married, but in the back of our minds, we know that if it gets too bad, we can always get a divorce. Kind of like, "I believe that this airplane is safe, but just in case, I've brought along a parachute. If I don't like it, if the ride gets too rough, I can always bail out."

See the similarities? If your spouse doesn't give you goose bumps anymore, go find someone who will. If God doesn't rock your world every time you pray, go find something that will. If your husband doesn't pay attention to you, go flirt with another guy. If God doesn't answer your prayers the way you want him to, worship something that will. If your wife asks you to do something you don't want to do, walk out the door. When God tells you to do something you don't want to do, turn your back on him.

3. Watch how you date and how you break up now.

This is a recording. Are you getting the picture? If you are a cheat now, you will be more prone to cheat later. If you have no physical control now, you probably won't later. If another person broke up with someone else to go out with you, wouldn't you be concerned that they might do the same to you?

4. Be a person of integrity. Keep your word.

Honor your promises. It is more important to *be* the right person than to *find* the right person. Someday you will stand in the front of a church building and covenant with your husband or wife. You will promise to always be there, to always love, always be faithful, regardless of circumstances—health, money, good times and bad. To keep those promises, you must be a person of integrity. Keep your word.

5. Turn your dating relationship over to God.

Whatever happens in this relationship, it must be pleasing to God. Start praying for your future husband or wife now. Remember the "Adam method" in chapter one? Rest and trust in the Lord and he will bring to you what you need at just the right time. (Remember, Adam went to sleep trusting God and woke up to a great surprise.) Until that right time, God will supply all that you need.

Before I close this chapter, let me address two groups of people: First, those of you who come from divorced homes, don't close this book and announce to your parents, "Jim says you're a big sinner. You shouldn't have gotten a divorce!" Why? First of all, I don't need 100 phone calls tomorrow. More importantly, you probably don't know all of the true facts involved in your parents' divorce, and no one is in any position to judge. You need to leave that to your parents and God. No one who has gone through the pain of divorce needs more guilt piled on them. What they do need is love, forgiveness and support—especially from their children. One relationship has failed; don't let it ruin another. If you need help healing from your parents' divorce, get it from a counselor, a minister or a trusted friend.

The second group are those readers who have already violated the sexual covenant that was supposed to wait for marriage. I've said it a thousand times. My job is not to point a finger at anyone. My job is to point the way to Jesus Christ, and the Jesus I read about in the Bible and know personally is a God who is more than willing to forgive and purify your life again. Forgiveness is available by giving your life to God and having the death of Jesus serve as payment for your sins. My favorite verse is Romans 5:8: "God demonstrates his own love for us in this: While we were still sinners, Christ died for us."

At the moment of your deepest need, God embraces you. God

is a big God and he can handle your sin, but you and he need to get that worked out right away. (We'll be talking more about forgiveness later.)

Getting Personal

1. *How is marriage a "picture" of our relationship with Jesus?*

2. *How does Jesus protect us and provide what we need?*

3. *How do we "protect and provide for" Jesus?*

4. *Why is Satan so anti-marriage and family?*

5. *What is a covenant? How does one get out of a covenant?*

6. *Why would God command us to marry (and date) only other Christians? (2 Corinthians 6:14).*

7. *What does, "If you cheat now, you will be more prone to cheat later" mean?*

8. *What is the "Adam method" of dating?*

Choices of the Heart

9

Choices of the Heart

We love to play Nintendo at my house. My son Jordan is the best. In each game there is a situation and Jordan must find the provided way through the castle or the maze or whatever. Sometimes it's easy and obvious. Why? Because he's been there before! But sometimes it takes more time to find the way out. However, there's always a way. The game would be pointless and not much fun if the designers of the game had our little electronic hero walk into a room where there was no escape or chance of survival. The key to Nintendo is to see the problem and make the right choice. The same is true with God. There is always a choice.

It's like that old monkey trap story. (I saw this on the Discovery Channel late one night.) The monkey hunter drills a hole in a coconut and, in full view of the monkey, places a coin inside. The hunter then leaves, allowing the curious monkey to come down out of the tree to retrieve the coin. The problem arises when the monkey can't remove his coin-filled fist from the tiny hole. The monkey wants to be free but he also wants what's inside the coconut. When the hunter returns, rather than letting go of the coin and escaping, the screaming, greedy monkey ends up losing both the coin and his freedom.

Sometimes, we find ourselves in situations where we feel there are no options, no way out. But the fact is, we *a) don't like the available options, b) don't really want to get out* or *c) choose to stay in danger.*

It's like the guy who was awakened in the night by someone pounding on his front door. He answered it to find a sheriff there with a warning, "You need to get to high ground, a flood is coming." The man responded, "I'm not worried, God will take care of me." In the middle of the night, the water flooded his house so he had to climb onto his roof to escape the rising water. A man came by in a boat and shouted, "I'm on my way to dry land, do you want a ride?" "No," the man responded, "God will save me." The water continued to rise until the man was standing on the top of his chimney. A helicopter flew by and hovered over him. The pilot shouted, "We're on our way to dry land. Do you want a ride?" "No," the man replied, "God will save me." The man died. Standing before God on Judgment Day, he asked God, "Why did you let me die? I thought you would save me." God replied, "I tried. I sent you a warning, a boat and a helicopter."

I was watching a program on the Discovery Channel (I watch it a lot) which explained how elephants are trained to be in the circus. As I watched, the trainer chained the baby elephant to a tree. For hours, the baby elephant struggled to break free, but he couldn't break the big chain. Finally, in his elephant mind, he decided, "I cannot get free; I cannot break the chain." Years later, as an adult, although now physically able to snap the chain and walk away, the elephant cannot break free from the mental idea of being a prisoner. So with a tiny stake in the ground and a small chain, the elephant remains a prisoner. A simple change of mind and he could be free.

Recently, I polled about 200 high school students with this question: "What is the top pressure or subject or issue in your life that you have to deal with as a high school student?" I received many different answers, but on nearly every list, one subject kept coming up: "sexual pressure and lust." So in this chapter, we are going to talk about how to deal with lust, looking at the problem, identifying your choices and figuring out how God might be trying to save you from "drowning."

Back to the Bible. Here's the situation: Jesus is talking to religious people who, on the outside, look like they have it all together. But Jesus has a way of seeing through all of the hypocrisy and the "public masks" that people wear and addressing the real issues of a person's life. So he says,

"'You have heard that it was said, "Do not commit adultery." But I tell you that anyone who looks at a woman lustfully has already committed adultery with her in his heart'" (Matthew 5:27, 28).

Now, I don't know why these people showed up to hear Jesus, but I don't think many of them came to have their lives changed. Maybe they came for some good advice. Maybe they came to be reassured that they were basically good people—you know, like why many of us go to church. But Jesus cuts through all of the garbage and says, "Hey, on the outside, you obey all of the rules and standards. You have everybody faked into thinking you are a nice, holy person, but on the inside, you're a mess. OK, so you're not out there sleeping around or having sex, but inside, you sure want to. You think about it all the time, you fantasize about it. In your mind and your heart, you've already done it; and in God's eyes, you're just as guilty."

I think every guy, and probably every girl, in the crowd turned pale, swallowed hard and tried not to puke. See, on the outside, everything looked fine, but they knew what went on inside their minds and hearts—and they realized at that moment that God knew as well.

Now, I want to clarify something. God never condemns a person for being tempted. Temptation is not a sin. The Bible says that Jesus was tempted in every way we are, yet he didn't sin (Hebrews 4:15). See, the sin part begins when you take the temptation and pursue it. Jesus had the same choices we have, he had every opportunity to sin, but he chose each time to pursue the right course of action.

Please understand, when you become a Christian, God does not expect guys to ignore the fact that girls have attractive figures, great hair or soft skin or for girls to ignore the fact that guys have biceps, dimples, great legs or that "they're cute," nor does he expect you not to think about the fact that one day, you want to have sex. The fact is, we are sexual people and ignoring that fact only frustrates you.

What God is saying is that you have within you a very powerful force—sexuality—which in the right place is going to be awesome, but when it is pursued in the wrong manner can cost you your soul. So, Jesus gives us the solution to our dilemma. Here's what he says:

> "If your right eye causes you to sin, gouge it out and throw it away. It is better for you to lose one part of your body than for your whole body to be thrown into hell. And if your right hand causes you to sin, cut it off and

*throw it away. It is better for you to lose one part of your
body than for your whole body to go into hell'" (Matthew
5:29, 30).*

Do you know why a doctor would amputate a body part? The
infected, dying part is removed to preserve the rest of the
healthy body, to give the body a chance for recovery. In some
parts of the world, like the Middle East, authorities sever or
cut out the offending body part used in the crime as punish-
ment, as well as for the criminal's "own good." The reasoning
is that maybe if the criminal doesn't have that part, he won't
commit this crime again.

Now, we're talking about lust. Before you panic, be assured
that I don't think Jesus is suggesting that if you struggle with
lust, you should cut off your sex organs. (Shoo . . . thank good-
ness!) Remember, action comes from the overflow of the heart.
It's a spiritual problem, not a physical one, but it is played out
on a physical level.

What *is* Jesus saying then? He's saying, "Hey, you are a sexual
person. You are surrounded by tempting situations and circumstances. Be careful. They can damage your heart." *When*, not *if*,
you are tempted to lust, go to the source of the problem and . . .

1. Cut it out of your life *(whatever "it" is).*

He doesn't say, "Try harder! Conquer it! Defeat it." He says to go
to the source and eliminate its presence from your life. Bring it

to a close, whether it's pornography, inappropriate music choices, dressing improperly or hanging out with the wrong crowd. Sometimes you may have to gouge it out. It won't be easy and it will take a conscious effort. Don't be ignorant. Temptation to sin will not leave easily. Whatever "it" is will fight to stay. It may be a painful process, like cutting off an infected limb that threatens to contaminate and kill the entire body.

2. Throw it away.

Put space between the two of you. Get away from it. Once you remove its presence from your life, stay out of situations that will replace it with more of the same.

Pursuing a temptation is always a choice. It is better to lose something major for something better. There are things that are important and things that are more important. I like how the missionary Jim Elliot put it. He said, "He is no fool who gives what he cannot keep to gain what he cannot lose." There are things that are more important than what promises to make you feel good right now.

You say, "I can't. I can't stop. I can't turn my back on this part of my life. I don't have the strength to just stop." Listen: "No temptation has seized you except what is common to man. And God is faithful; he will not let you be tempted beyond what you can bear. But when you are tempted, he will provide a way out so that you can stand up under it" (1 Corinthians 10:13). God will let you know how to stop.

For example, you get on the Internet. It's so easy to click to some bad stuff. But before you get there, God will warn you, "Get out of here! Don't click on that!" You can hear him. You pick up a magazine. You will hear God's voice say, "Don't open it! Put it down! Don't look in there!" Or you are watching a movie scene. God will make it as plain as day: "Turn it off and walk away!"

The other day I was watching a rather well-known movie about a big ship that sinks. (Hmmm, I wonder what it was?) Anyway, I had been told that there is one scene where a woman is being painted . . . and she is "nekk-id." As I watched the movie, it was obvious when the scene was about to occur. Just before the scene, I "heard" God tell me, "Jim, now would be a good time to go and get some popcorn." My response was, "Lord, I'm not hungry . . . for popcorn." Finally, there she was on the screen. As clear as day, I knew that God wanted me to look at the floor, to which I responded, "No, Lord, I want to look." I heard God and made my choice. *My* choice. God always gives you a choice. I chose the wrong thing.

Jesus says in John 16:8 that it is God, not some preacher, who will convict you, tell you what is right and wrong and exactly what you need to do. That voice, that conviction is called the Holy Spirit. The Holy Spirit is the part of God that draws people to himself to become Christians and once they are, lives in them and guides their lives. Part of that guidance is "Get out of here! Walk away! Don't open it! Do this instead."

But just like Adam and Eve in the Garden, following God's

voice is always your choice. You choose. We all do. We rationalize that "This isn't *that* bad. I can handle it. It doesn't affect me." We explain it away: "It's not that big of a deal; I've seen worse." We minimize it, we compare it: "This is *nothing* compared to what some people do!" We deny it: "I *like* it. I want to be a part of this." We tell God to mind his own business. We choose the "tree," just like Adam and Eve did.

You say, "Well, why doesn't God just take away the temptation?" God will never take away your position to choose. To take away all of your choices so that God is the only option isn't love; it's dictatorship. God allows you to choose because he loves it when you choose him and his way.

Let's close with some really practical suggestions on dealing with lust. Honestly, many of us set ourselves up for a fall. How can we overcome lust?

1. Walk away.

In a world that devours lust, where sex is the main marketing tool of everything from perfume to dog food (as if using any particular dog food will make you "sexy"), walking away from lustful situations will never be easy, convenient or popular. Walking away from sexually tempting situations is counterculture; it's alternative; it's difficult. And honestly, you can't eliminate every tempting situation from your life.

I'm not suggesting that if you see a seductive billboard (like

Hooters' sign), you cover your eyes. That could cause some serious car accidents. Or if a guy takes off his shirt in P.E. class, you run out of the gym. Can you imagine? It would be hilarious if you walked down the hallway at school and you saw guys sticking their heads in lockers. "What's wrong?" you ask. They respond, "I just saw a girl with breasts walking down the hallway and I'm trying not to lust." (On the other hand, maybe it would help.)

But even if you can't escape all situations where there might be sexual temptations, you can choose to avoid the obvious ones. You know that every time you go to certain places, you are tempted to think or pursue lustful thoughts or actions. (You know exactly what I mean—certain kinds of movies, magazines, web pages, parties.) Before you even go there, you know what you are going to find. So, simply choose not to go.

I've heard it said, "If you are an alcoholic, stay out of bars." If you are a normal human being with normal sexual desires and interest, stay out of obvious places designed to arouse those desires. It's not going to be easy. Have you ever noticed that when you go on a diet, suddenly all you can think about is food? Learning new habits and letting go of old ones is difficult. But it starts with a choice that you can make right now, which leads to:

2. Clean house.

Be honest: you voluntarily expose yourself to most of the things that cause you to lust. Though it might be a struggle, you could choose to eliminate them, to cut them off and throw them away. Many of us simply need to clean house. Literally. Look around your room, your car, your locker from a "God perspective." God will tell you what needs to go. Magazines and pictures designed to stimulate. Articles about how to sexually satisfy your partner. (Listen, there is only one way: A Christ-centered marriage. There are no secret techniques, spots or games which can replace that.) What is in your life that needs to go? You know! Now choose.

3. Dress the part.

Ladies, guys need your help on this next one. Remember the differences in guys and girls mentioned in chapter two? Here is one more. Guys are more apt to be tempted by visual stimulation. Girls tend to be more attracted to relational stimulation—compliments, conversation, courtesy. God did a wonderful thing when he created you girls, but we guys need some help. We need for you to dress with modesty. When you put on something that shows every curve and feature of your body, in our weakness, it puts us in a tempting situation.

Paul wrote in 1 Corinthians 10:32 to do your best not to "cause anyone to stumble," meaning, try your best to avoid creating a situation where someone else might be tempted to mess up. A few verses earlier, he urged, "Nobody should seek his own good [or rights], but the good of others" (10:24). Ladies, help us out by dressing to please God rather than men.

4. Choose God's way out.

God never asks you to do more than what he is willing to support (1 Corinthians 10:13). There is a difference between "I can't" and "I won't," as we learned with the monkey that got his hand caught in the coconut, or the elephant tied to the chain. With God, it's like playing Nintendo with someone who's already won, like following a guide who leads the way. But he always leaves the choice up to you: follow or go your own way. It's a choice of the heart.

Getting Personal

1. What does the statement, "With God, it always involves a choice," mean?

2. Obviously, God doesn't want you hacking body parts off, so what does it mean to cut off your hand and throw it away if it causes you to sin?

3. Jim Elliot said, "He is no fool who gives what he cannot keep to gain what he cannot lose." How would this apply to the choices involved in a young person's sexual temptations and choices?

4. What are some things in your life that you need to "lose," to "cut off and throw away"?

5. In the final part of this chapter we talked about the weakness that many guys have in the area of visual stimulation. Why would it be reasonable to ask young women to dress modestly because of this? Why isn't it just the guys' problem?

6. Is there some area of your life where you are torn between "I can't" and "I won't"? What is God telling you to do about it?

What About
Homosexuality?

10

What About Homosexuality?

What causes someone to be a homosexual? I get asked this question a lot and my answer is, "I don't know!" There, isn't that wise? But the fact is, I've never met anyone who can say absolutely, "this" causes someone to be homosexual. There are a lot of ideas: an overdominant parent, an overly passive parent, an abusive situation, an over- or underdeveloped section of the brain. All of these have been presented as possible causes of homosexuality.

I simply don't know. I have met people who can say definitively, "This is when I started to feel gay." On the other hand, I have met people who claim they have "always" had these feelings.

But there are many things I don't understand. I don't know why one person has a tendency to be an alcoholic, while another person never struggles in the same area. I don't know why one person can control his anger and another person can't. I don't know why one person can quit smoking while another can't.

Here is what I do understand: we all struggle with temptation. Yours might be heterosexual temptation. Hers might be homosexual temptation. You can argue that one is normal and one isn't, but the truth is that if either temptation is acted on in an improper fashion, it becomes sin. And remember, God doesn't grade on a curve. Sin is sin!

Temptation isn't the sin. Let me repeat that: temptation is *not* a sin. Pursuing and acting out the temptation is the sin. In the Bible, homosexual temptation (or any other temptation) is not

119

condemned as sin. It becomes sin when the man or woman actually puts these feelings into practice and begins to carry them out. Let's see what the Bible has to say:

"'If a man lies [that is an action, a verb] with a man as one lies with a woman, both of them have done what is detestable. They must be put to death; their blood will be on their own heads'" (Leviticus 20:13).

"Do you not know that the wicked will not inherit the kingdom of God? Do not be deceived: Neither the sexually immoral nor idolaters nor adulterers nor male prostitutes nor homosexual offenders [action] nor thieves nor the greedy nor drunkards nor slanderers nor swindlers will inherit the kingdom of God. And that is what some of you were. But you were washed, you were sanctified, you were justified in the name of the Lord Jesus Christ and by the Spirit of our God" (1 Corinthians 6:9-11).

"Therefore God gave them over [action] in the sinful desires of their hearts to sexual impurity for the degrading [action] of their bodies with one another. They exchanged [action] the truth of God for a lie, and worshiped and served created things rather than the Creator—who is forever praised. Amen.

"Because of this, God gave them over to shameful lusts*. Even their women exchanged [action] natural relations for unnatural ones. In the same way the men also abandoned natural relations with women and were inflamed with lust* [action] for one another. Men com-

mitted indecent acts [action] *with other men, and received in themselves the due penalty for their perversion" (Romans 1:24-27).*

(*Lust is a fantasy activity where the individual engages in sexual activity in mind and heart—"if I could, I would"—and eventually acts on it.)

There is a great difference between "struggling with temptation" and active involvement. Take a look at 1 Corinthians 6:11 which states that the people in question "used" to be offenders. That means that they don't "offend" anymore. It doesn't mean that the struggles are all gone. Paul himself states that as long as we are in the flesh, there will always be struggles. But with God's help, those struggles—with homosexual temptation only one of many—can be kept under control. And, with the power of God, homosexuality *can* be overcome. Let me give you an example that might help.

One Sunday night in my church when I was growing up, a man came forward at the end of the service. He began with, "Hi, my name is John and I'm an alcoholic." He confessed that his earlier life had been ruled by alcohol. It had cost him everything dear to him—his marriage, his children, his career, his reputation. But then he accepted Christ as his Lord and Savior, and by grace, he hadn't had a drink in nearly 10 years.

Was he still an alcoholic? Yes, he was. He knew that with one drink, he could be swept back into a lifestyle that would kill him. But because of God's power, he was no longer an alcoholic "offender." I have met a few recovering alcoholics who have accepted Jesus and never had a craving for alcohol again. However, for most alcoholics, it is a daily struggle. One day at a time with God's help, they turn away from the bottle.

Many times it's the same with the homosexual. I believe that God has the power to totally, instantly deliver a person from homosexual temptation. But my experience has been much more, "Hi, my name is John and I'm a homosexual. With God's help, I haven't acted (offended) on those feelings in five years, but it's a daily struggle."

If you struggle with homosexual feelings (or someone close to you does), the best thing you can do would be the following:

Realize that God loves you no matter how you feel, what you've done or how deep you are in.
No matter what, God has not given up on you. Even if he hates what you are doing, he does not hate you. He does not think that you are weird, strange or gross. And he wants to help.

Realize that sexual temptation is one of the most powerful forces in the universe.
You cannot overcome this by yourself. Your own willpower is not enough. Find a Christian leader or friend you can trust who will keep you accountable, ask you tough questions and love you no matter what.

Here are a few examples of some tough questions that you need to be asked:

- Have you voluntarily looked at something you shouldn't have?
- Have you physically pursued acting out your homosexual temptation with another person or even through lustful thoughts?
- Is there anything in your possession that needs to be banished from your presence?
- Have you made good choices this week in this area of temptation? Have you made mistakes? What do you need to do to avoid the same mistakes?

Remember, 1 Corinthians 10:13 promises that God will not let you be tempted beyond what you can stand. That's a promise. Listen:

"No temptation has seized you except what is common to man. And God is faithful; he will not let you be tempted beyond what you can bear. But when you are tempted, he will also provide a way out so that you can stand up under it."

It says that God will always provide you with a way out of temptation. Be honest: many times when you find yourself in a tempting situation, you have voluntarily placed yourself there, especially in a sexually tempting situation. This is why accountability is so important. I know I can find ways to justify and sneak my way right back into a situation that I know is wrong. An accountability partner or leader can lovingly see what we are doing and gently (or firmly) call us on the carpet and steer us back in the right direction. Let me repeat this: sexual temptation is probably the toughest one out there. You cannot overcome this alone. It will take a lot of commitment, the work of the Holy Spirit, the help of an accountability partner—and, of course . . .

Realize the power of prayer.
You need to pray—a lot! This is going to be tough. You are going to have to get really close to God to make it through this tough time. Overcoming any sexual sin is usually not a matter of praying on Monday and being cured on Tuesday. This struggle might be with you for the rest of your life. But God's grace is sufficient to see you through. The apostle Paul said,

> *"To keep me from becoming conceited because of these surpassingly great revelations, there was given me a thorn in my flesh, a messenger of Satan, to torment me. Three times I pleaded with the Lord to take it away from me. But he said to me, 'My grace is sufficient for you, for my power is made perfect in weakness.' Therefore I will boast all the more gladly about my weaknesses, so that Christ's power may rest on me. That is why, for Christ's sake, I delight in weaknesses, in insults, in hardships, in persecutions, in difficulties. For when I am weak, then I am strong"*
> *(2 Corinthians 12:7-10).*

If you (or someone you know) is struggling with homosexuality you might want to contact Exodus International for more help on this subject. This organization was founded in 1976 and its primary purpose is to "proclaim that freedom from homosexuality is possible through repentance and faith in Jesus Christ as Savior and Lord." Exodus seeks to motivate and train Christians to restore sexual wholeness to men and women who desire to overcome their homosexuality.

For more information call them at (206) 784-7799 or visit their web site at www.exodusintl.org.

The next question we need to address is: *How should a Christian respond to a person involved in homosexuality?*

Every once in a while, it seems that Christians decide that a few important controversial issues will become a litmus test to see if a person really is a Christian. If they believe "this way," then they are a real Christian. If they believe "the other way," then their whole salvation is called into question. In the last few years, abortion and homosexuality have become a sort of litmus test on these issues. (A litmus test is a scientific test that indicates whether a chemical solution is acid or alkaline; in life terms, it tests whether something is true to the issue in question.)

I have opinions on this subject that probably will draw condemnation from many, but, oh well—here they are: First of all, I believe that both abortion and homosexual activity are sins. Is that clear enough? I don't want anything to water down that message. But I also believe that many times, Christians get into the habit of picking out certain sins to label as "really bad sins."

Remember when you were a little kid and you played army or capture the flag, or had a snowball fight, and your team was pinned down? The best way to escape was to send out a runner, usually the least liked person in the group, to draw the attention (and the snowballs) of the enemy. Then, while all of the focus was on the runner, the rest of the team would sneak out and capture the flag or run to safety.

I think that Christians play that game really well. If we can keep the focus on the "really bad sins," then maybe people won't notice our "little" sins. If we can get together and talk about the horrors of abortion or the abomination of homosexuality, then we can totally avoid the topics of our own materialism, judgmental attitudes, heterosexual lust, greed, hatred or unwholesome humor.

Another game we used to play as children was called, "Would You Rather?" In this game, you were given two choices (usually, both were pretty gross) and you had to choose. It went something like this: "Would you rather kiss Becky (a girl in my third grade class who vomited at the least suggestion) or wear Eddie's underwear for an entire hour (Eddie, another third grader, had the annoying habit of "soiling himself" at least once a week)? Those were the choices. Gross, I know, but hey, we were in the third grade and those were the worst choices we could think of!

If I chose Becky, the teasing would start: "Jim loves Becky! Are you going to marry her? Jim and Becky sitting in a tree, k-i-s-s-i-n-g . . . ." If I chose Eddie, people would gasp in disbelief: "You'd actually wear his underwear? Ooh, gross!" Either way, I'd start justifying my answer. "Yeah, well, at least I didn't kiss Becky—she has green vomit stuck in her teeth!" Or, "at least it's not as bad as wearing dirty undies!"

Chapter Ten

I know, you think I've lost it—"What is he talking about?" Don't you see? We do the same thing! Let me give you a choice: "Would you rather go to Hell for being a homosexual offender, or for being greedy and selfish?" Who cares? You go to Hell in either case. And both sins are forgivable through the same and only way—Jesus Christ.

Hey, Christians, get off your seats of judgment and realize that we are all in the same boat! A certain sin might gross you out more than another, but nowhere does God mention "grading on a curve" and you are in the same situation unless you have Jesus as your Savior and Lord. There are no "really bad sins." There is just sin. And Jesus is the only solution to any sin.

Allow me to talk about another response. Recently, I was watching a video that contained a conversation between two people who had recently found out that one of their friends was gay. One of the girls watching the video with me made the comment, "If I found out that my friend was gay, we just couldn't be friends anymore." My instant response to that was, "Well, then, you just closed the best door to that person ever finding their way out of that lifestyle."

I'm finding that we frequently do the same: when we are confronted by a sin that we don't understand, don't know what to do to escape, feel threatened or repulsed by, we simply abandon the situation and go find a safer yard to play in. In other words, we run.

Instead, look at the example of Jesus. Time and time again, we

127

find Jesus eating lunch, attending weddings and parties or just "hanging out" with sinners (whom he referred to at worst, as "sick people needing a doctor" and at best, as "friends"). Every time—every time—you find Jesus talking to "sinners," you find him loving them, restoring them, forgiving them. You never find him yelling at them (they've had enough people yelling at them), rehashing their mistakes with them (they knew what was wrong in their life) or even preaching long sermons to them. He just loved them . . . and when the time was right, he called them to something better (Zacchaeus, the woman caught in adultery, Peter the fisherman).

Let me ask you: Who has a better chance of introducing a homosexual to the love, grace and forgiveness of Jesus Christ: the friend who is acting like Jesus, showing unconditional love even when disapproving of the lifestyle or the midwestern preacher who makes a habit of showing up at the funerals of AIDS victims with a big sign that says, "God hates fags"?

Frequently I have the opportunity to travel and speak. A few years ago, the subject of homosexuality came up. Without hesitation, I went right into my routine of speaking with a slight lisp and waving a limp wrist. It was good for an easy laugh from the crowd and I continued on without a second thought.

Later, after the auditorium had cleared, a young man in his early twenties approached me and said, "I know you didn't mean anything bad (he was very gracious), but the gay lifestyle has been a struggle for me for the last several years, and your jokes up there tonight . . . well, for me, it hurt. I already struggle with believing that God could love me. Comments like that make it even harder." Gulp. I begged for his forgiveness and pledged right there that would be the last time I would make a joke at the expense of someone trying to find Jesus.

Hate or humiliation has never brought anyone closer to Jesus. No one has ever been harassed into repentance. Love the sinner; hate the sin—that's what Jesus would do. That's what Jesus does. He did it for you. Aren't you glad? Where would you be if it were any different?

Getting Personal

1. *What do we mean when we say, "Temptation is not a sin"? When does it become a sin?*

2. *Why did Paul say that it was the "homosexual offender" who was a sinner and not just the homosexual?*

3. *For someone struggling to bring homosexual temptation under God's control, why is accountability with another person so vital and crucial? Do you think that accountability would help people who struggle with other sins as well?*

4. *Biblically, homosexual activity is condemned as sin. No argument there. But why do you think that Christians have singled out this one sin as the object of so much ridicule and persecution?*

5. What is the best way for the Christian to deal with the homosexual to give him/her the best way of learning of God's love and forgiveness and plan for his/her life?

6. Think about your actions and attitude toward the person who struggles with homosexuality. Have you made jokes about a situation that could cost someone's soul? Have you done anything that would make it harder for the homosexual to believe that hope can be found in Christ? Have you done what Jesus would do? What are some changes you might need to make in your own life?

What About Masturbation?

11

What About Masturbation?

OK, I never thought that I would ever talk openly about masturbation, let alone dedicate a chapter of a book to it. But it's a huge question out there. And a popular one—but no one will talk about it. So I will.

Have you ever had one of those nights in youth group meeting when people submit anonymous questions on slips of paper, then the leader draws out the various slips and reads and addresses the question? I can almost guarantee the "masturbation question" is in nearly every pile of papers. And you can always tell when the leader gets to it. He or she panics—and sometimes slips the paper into a pocket and draws out another slip.

Here is the question: Is it a sin to masturbate? (Right now, aren't you a little nervous that someone is going to peek over your shoulder to see what you're reading?) Anyway, here we go: Masturbation is not specifically mentioned in the Bible. Some people have connected masturbation with the "sin of Onan." Onan was this guy in the Old Testament who was supposed to father a child for his dead brother's wife. It was an Old Testament law. He didn't want to do this, so to avoid impregnating his sister-in-law, he "spilled his seed on the ground." Here, read it for yourself:

> "At that time, Judah left his brothers and went down to stay with a man of Adullam named Hirah. There Judah met the daughter of a Canaanite man named Shua. He married her and lay with her; she became pregnant and gave birth to a son, who was named Er. She conceived again and gave birth to a son and named him Onan. She gave birth to still another son and named him Shelah. It

was at Kezib that she gave birth to him.

"Judah got a wife for Er, his firstborn, and her name was Tamar. But Er, Judah's firstborn, was wicked in the LORD's sight; so the LORD put him to death.

"Then Judah said to Onan, 'Lie with your brother's wife and fulfill your duty to her as a brother-in-law to produce offspring for your brother.' But Onan knew that the off-spring would not be his; so whenever he lay with his broth-er's wife, he spilled his semen on the ground to keep from producing offspring for his brother. What he did was wicked in the LORD's sight; so he put him to death also" (Genesis 38:1-10).

Some people have speculated that Onan masturbated before having sex with Tamar. Others conclude that what Onan did was not masturbation, but *coitus interruptus*, the act of remov-ing his penis from Tamar's vagina just before ejaculation so that no semen would be available to fertilize Tamar's ovum. (By the way, this is not the most effective form of birth control.) In any case, Onan was condemned, not for the sexual act, but for fail-ing to obey the law of providing for his brother's wife.

Masturbation is the physical act of stimulating one's own sexu-al organs for pleasure. There are a ton of rumors and old wives' tales surrounding masturbation, things like, "If you masturbate, you will go blind or grow hair on odd places of your body." I think most of these tales were started by well-meaning people attempting to frighten others away from the "horrible sin of masturbation." Well, you can relax. Masturbation will not harm your eyesight nor cause any unsightly body hair, and, masturbation is not a sin. However, it does place you in a dangerous and opportune position to sin. Allow me to explain.

Usually, masturbation is accompanied with lust.

As we have already discussed, Jesus comes right out and condemns lust (Matthew 5:28). When a man or woman is masturbating, he or she usually is physically acting out a sexual, lustful thought or fantasy in the mind even if not with another person. Lust is a sin. Lust is an out-of-control thought. Most of the time, masturbation is the physical expression of that thought.

Masturbation gives an unfair comparison.

Real life (your future spouse) has a difficult time competing with a wild fantasy life. This is one of the dangers of pornography. It provides expectations that real life just can't compete with. You create in your mind what you think or expect the real thing to be like; then, if it's not, disappointment results.

God commands us to be in control of our bodies.

Paul says that we have to keep them in check. We are to tell our bodies what they will do (1 Corinthians 9:25-27). We are not animals controlled by instincts or drives. We are the only creation who can make choices and whom God promises to empower to overcome temptation (1 Corinthians 10:13).

Now, I am not saying that it is a sin to have sexual thoughts. We are sexual beings. Our bodies were made to have sex. God wants us to have sex—at the right time. We have hormones pulsing through our bodies. And we notice other people and are attracted to them. The problem comes when those natural feelings drag us into activities and thoughts that become sinful.

For example: You are a human. You are sexual. You have sexual feelings. Someday you want to have sex with your husband or wife. You wonder what that will be like. You look forward to that day. This is all good. The problem comes when you begin to fantasize about having sex with a certain person. When you have sex with him or her in your mind while possibly stimulating yourself, something good (natural sexuality) crosses over into sin. (Girls, you know this is not just a guy thing; it goes both ways.)

If you struggle with masturbation, let me suggest the following:

1. Be careful what you are placing before your eyes.

Like I said earlier, everything is "ready and wanting to go." To place yourself in stimulating circumstances is like mixing fire and gasoline. If you are struggling with lust, keep yourself away from places and circumstances that get those juices flowing. You know exactly what I mean. God's Spirit will make it very clear to you: shut the magazine, leave the theater, turn off the computer, walk away from the situation. The choice is always yours.

2. Talk to a same-sex Christian leader.

If you think you could never do that, remember, they have struggled with the exact same feelings and temptations. We all have. We are all in the same boat. Most activities, especially ones involving strong drives like sex, can be kept in control only by accountability. Speaking as a longtime youth minister, I would not be the least bit shocked or embarrassed to sit with a high school guy and talk about this subject. But just like any sexual situation, you are going to need accountability to bring it into check. Now, you can always lie, but when you know that someone who really cares about you is going to ask you, "Did you lust, did you masturbate this week?"—it makes a difference and may be exactly what you need to give you the strength to keep things under control.

3. Don't walk around carrying guilt.

"Oh, I'm an awful person because I've masturbated; I must be a bad Christian, a pervert, a sex fiend." No, you are a Christian struggling in a lifelong battle with the flesh. I don't want to minimize any sin, but realize that all sin is forgivable through Jesus Christ. If you struggle with masturbation, the secret is not to keep making pledges such as, "OK, that was the last time." But it is a huge flag that you need to turn more and more of this area of your life over to Jesus for his lordship and control.

4. Fill your mind with Christ.

Don't ignore the fact that you have sexual feelings, but the more you are filled with Christ and his thoughts, the more available his power will be to keep things in control.

Paul writes in Philippians 4:8, "Finally, brothers, whatever is true, whatever is noble, whatever is right, whatever is pure, whatever is lovely, whatever is admirable—if anything is excellent or praiseworthy—think about such things" and in Colossians 3:2, he instructs us to "Set your minds on things above, not on earthly things." The more your mind is full of the things of God, the less room there is for the stuff that drags you down.

It's like that whole "Just Say No" to drugs campaign from a few years ago. Don't you wish it was that easy? I don't mean to sound too simplistic, but you can't say "no" to anything until you say "yes" to something better. I frequently get asked, "How far can I go?", meaning, "What things can I get away with sexually before I cross some line that will tick God off?" My response usually is that while I will give you some guide-lines, you are asking the wrong question.

Picture it this way. You have a big circle. In the center of this circle is the perfect will of God, his perfect plan—the bull's-eye. Right at the edge of the circle is a huge drop-off down to Hell. Most of the questions that we ask are like, "How far is too far? Can I be a Christian and still . . . drink? smoke? watch these movies? listen to this music? do these sexual things?

masturbate?" Wouldn't the better questions be, "How close to the center can I get (to God's perfect plan)? Does this activity bring me closer to the edge or the center? Am I trying to get as close to God as possible, or get away with as much as possible before I 'tick him off'?"

Is masturbation a sin? No, but at best, it is a dangerous activity with the potential to place you in a very compromising and sinful situation. Should you masturbate? Well, our goal as Christians is to be as close to God and in the center of his will as possible. We are to "fix our eyes on him." He is our goal, our prize, our example and our commander. The more we say "yes" to him, the more our "no's" and "should's" take care of themselves.

Getting Personal

etting Personal

1. *If masturbation isn't the issue (sin), what is?*

2. *What are some of the dangers of masturbation (excluding blindness and huge growths of body hair)?*

3. *Why would it be important to talk to a trusted person about your struggle with masturbation—or any other temptation? Why isn't the solution to sin to simply "Just Say No"?*

4. *It would be easy to justify masturbation by simply claiming that it doesn't "hurt anybody." But it does involve another person. Who?*

What About Interracial Dating?

12

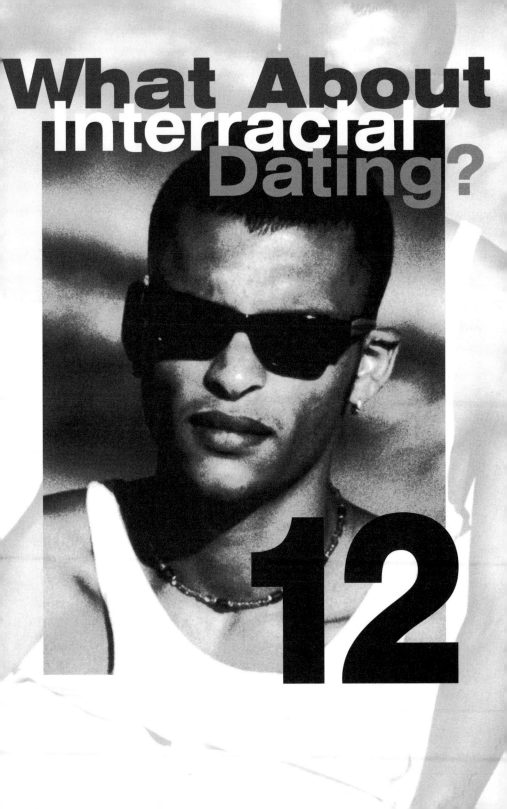

What About Interracial Dating?

Interracial dating and marriage, the romantic involvement of two people of different races, is a growing issue in the United States. Just a few years ago, two people of different races dating, let alone marrying, was very unusual, especially in many churches. But times are changing, and, as Christians, we must not look to the world or what is currently a fad, but to the Bible, for our instruction.

The most frequently used argument on the negative side of the interracial issue is Paul's command that Christians not be "unequally yoked." "Do not be yoked together with unbelievers. For what do righteousness and wickedness have in common? Or what fellowship can light have with darkness?" (2 Corinthians 6:14).

The fact is that this command is strictly a spiritual command. A believer should not date or marry a nonbeliever. This isn't my idea or even the apostle Paul's idea. It is God's command. The light and darkness that Paul addresses has nothing to do with skin tones, but the condition of the heart (that is, unless you think that one skin tone has an exclusive corner on righteousness). To be truthful, the Bible does not even speak to the issue of interracial dating and marriage, and where the Bible is silent, we should also be silent.

The closest thing that I have found in the Bible is in the story of Moses. After Moses fled from Egypt, he came to a well in the land of Midian and met up with Jethro, a priest, who gave Moses one of his daughters in marriage. By tradition, it is believed that the people of Midian were a dark-skinned people (did you see the movie *The Prince of Egypt*?). If Jethro, whose name literally means "friend of God," was a priest, we can assume that the members of his entire family were believers. So, Moses and his wife met the criteria of being equally yoked—not based on the color of their skin, but by faith.

It is not a sin to date or marry a person of a different race. The most important issue is that the person you date and marry be a believer and follower of Jesus Christ. Having said that, let me also include this caution:

Dating and marriage are tough. They are tough when you have everything going for you: similar backgrounds, supportive families, supportive friends, secure finances, common interests. I believe that with Christ, all things are possible, and I know several interracial couples who are doing very well. But please know, introducing the multiracial issue into a relationship brings many new obstacles and hurdles into play. It makes something that is tough even tougher. I'm not saying, "Don't." I'm saying, "Be careful."

I also think we need to be careful to remember a few other things. I have had the opportunity to participate in several foreign mission projects and to visit different cultures. As a sociology student, I find studying these different people groups very interesting.

For example, in India, many marriages are still arranged by the parents. Popular opinion in India is that the parents know best and should be trusted to make the best decision for their children. Romance and personal happiness are on the list, but those factors aren't the primary consideration in making a match. Is this right or wrong? It's neither. It's cultural. The Bible has absolutely nothing to say about dating or arranged marriages. As a matter of fact, you could probably make a pretty strong argument supporting arranged marriages based on the number of biblical examples alone.

The Massai men of Kenya, a tribe in Africa, may pick a bride who may be 40 or 50 years younger than they are (again, arranged by her parents). Is this right or wrong? Neither. It's cultural. The Bible has nothing to say about the age difference of marriage partners. Now, we all have our opinions and personal tastes, but you can't turn age or race differences in marriage into a "sin" issue.

While we need to be sensitive to American culture and traditions, we need to be careful not to label them biblical or Christian standards as well. Just because "that's the way we do it in America" does not make it the only or right way. If you choose to date and marry a person of a different race, understand you will be taking on a tougher road. Because of many insensitive or small-minded people, you and your future children may face a difficult road as well—comments, stares, sneers or even open ridicule.

I am not trying to encourage or discourage anyone to or from interracial dating and marriage, but hear me loud and clear: **The most important thing in dating and marriage is a common trust and belief in Jesus Christ.** So . . . should you do it? That's between you, the other person and the Lord.

For my daughter, Alison, my prayer for her is to find a Christian husband who will love her, honor her and help her continue to grow as a Christian woman and realize her full potential in Christ. I want her husband to love her as Christ loves the church and for her to recognize his sacrificial leadership as she serves him. His race is a secondary factor compared to his faith.

Getting Personal

1. *What is the primary requirement that must be found in a person that a Christian is to date and/or marry?*

2. *Whose idea or command is this and why would it be given?*

3. *Why was it OK for Moses to marry a woman from Midian?*

4. *What are some obstacles or hurdles that a multiracial couple might encounter?*

5. *What if there are no Christians available you would want to date? What should you do?*

What If I've Already Messed Up?

13

What If I've Already Messed Up?

I want you to do something for me. Close your eyes (not yet, you won't be able to read) and for just a few seconds, picture yourself doing the worst sin you have ever committed. Ready . . . go.

It's pretty easy. At least for me it is. I know where my lowest point was. It is something that I am ashamed of, embarrassed by and have told very few people about (and no, I'm not going to confess it here in this book). Ever since it happened, it has haunted me. Oh, I'm a Christian and have heard all of the sermons about love and forgiveness, but I still am bothered by this incident.

I still have moments where I remember that I did it (I think this is one of the consequences of sin), but let me give you a couple of verses from the Bible and a children's story that have helped me understand God's perspective on what I did and what God has done for me since. Maybe it will help you as well. See if you can relate.

For some reason, I concluded that God would start caring for me and loving me when I turned my life over to him. Like, if I would give God my heart, make him my Lord and Savior, maybe get baptized, then God would look at me and love me—after I stopped doing bad stuff and started doing the things he wanted me to do, especially because I knew the right thing to do. I just hadn't been doing it. It's exactly the opposite.

Read these verses with me and I'll try to explain as we go through them:

> *"You see, at just the right time, when we were still powerless, Christ died for the ungodly. Very rarely will anyone die for a righteous man, though for a good man someone might possibly dare to die. But God demonstrates his own love for us in this: While we were still sinners, Christ died for us" (Romans 5:6-8).*

Did you catch that last verse? *While we were still sinners. Before* we stopped doing anything, while we were still doing it, God was already in love with us and doing what needed to be done in preparation for the day when we decided to follow him.

That's real love—to love us before we loved him back, while we were still sinners. When I was at my lowest point, Jesus looked at his Father and said, "There, that's why Jim needs me to die for him."

No matter what you've done, how badly you've blown it, God is not waiting on anything before he starts loving you. He already loves you—unconditionally, no matter what. And Jesus proved it by dying on a cross for you to buy the forgiveness that you would need for that sin you remembered at the beginning of this chapter.

The next question is, "What is my response to God's love and what Jesus has done for me?"

When I was about 10 years old, my parents bought me the *Chronicles of Narnia* by C.S. Lewis. I read them through and really liked them but I thought they were strictly fantasy books. But of course, they are so much more. Everything in them is symbolic of the kingdom of God.

When I was in college (and not living the Christian life as I should have been), I went to a Christian meeting at East Tennessee State University where a guy stood up and told a story taken from one of the Chronicles series, the story of a little boy named Eustace who had become a dragon. Eustace had walked into a dragon's cave, fallen in love with all of the dragon's treasure, begun to think dragon thoughts and shortly, the transformation was complete: Eustace became a dragon.

Being a dragon was fun for a while but eventually, the novelty wore off and being a dragon was, as you can imagine, pretty morbid. But he had a big problem: he didn't know how to "un-dragon" himself.

Have you ever felt like that? Man, I have. I felt like, "BOOM!" God was telling me, "He's talking about you." I had done things and become things I never imagined I would ever do or be. And here was the clincher: I didn't know how to undo them. All I knew how to do was to keep getting in deeper. I tried to rationalize that the stuff I had done wasn't that bad. I tried to ignore the things I'd done. But I knew I had become a dragon. Back to the story.

One day, Eustace, now a dragon, was walking through the woods and came face to face with the lion, Aslan, who symbolizes Jesus. The lion told the boy that he must "get undressed." Now, the dragon-boy wasn't wearing any clothes, just scales, but then he remembered that he was a dragon, a reptile. The lion must want him to shed his skin. So he did. He peeled off layers and layers of scales, always revealing another layer of green scales underneath.

Finally, after several attempted peelings, the lion said, "I must undress you." So Eustace lay down on his back and the lion came over, stuck his claws into the dragon's chest and started cutting and tearing away. He dug deep down inside and pulled Eustace, the boy, out of the cold green slime and plunged him into a cold stream. It hurt like anything, but when Eustace surfaced, he was a boy again.

OK, I'm sitting in this college classroom, listening to a fairy tale and crying like a baby. Why? Because that's what I needed. That's what I wanted. That's what it was going to take. I was going to have to go face to face with the lion—God. "God, here I am. This is what I've done: I've become a dragon."

So I did that. I was shaking like a leaf, but for the first time, I got real with God and asked for his forgiveness and help. And the awesome thing was, when I confessed my sin to God without excuse and asked for his forgiveness, I got it. He ripped off my "scales" and began to turn me into the man he had wanted me to be in the first place.

Oh, I'm not yet what I should be. But I know that I'm not what I was. And I know, that even when Satan tries to remind me of my past, I have God whispering in my ear of his love, his grace and forgiveness.

What about you? Have you become a dragon? Do you think you've gone too far—so far that there is no way back? Do you need to be "undragoned"? God is in the business of changing lives and forgiving sin. That's what he has done for me. No matter what you are or what you've done or even how many times you've done it, God's love, grace, and forgiveness are bigger and more than enough to take care of you. What's more, he really wants to do it. He is just waiting for you to ask.

What are you waiting for? He promises in 1 John 1:9, "If we confess our sins, he is faithful and just and will forgive us our sins and purify us from all righteousness." Go ahead—ask him.

Getting Personal

1. Why do so many people have such a hard time believing that God will truly forgive their sins?

2. Eustace, the boy in C.S. Lewis's tale, turned into a dragon because he filled his mind with "dragon thoughts." Have you ever felt like you have done things that you never thought you would?

3. What must you do or change in your life to get God to love you?

4. The Bible states that God wants all men to be saved (1 Timothy 2:4) and we know that God loves us just the way we are. Is that enough, or do we need to respond in some way? What is your response to the fact that God loves you and wants to forgive you?

5. Why do you think that Eustace couldn't "undragon" himself? Why did the lion have to do it for him?

6. How does Jesus "undragon" us?

Final **Thoughts**

Well, there it is. My first attempt at a book. I hope it helps. If you've gotten nothing else from this, I hope that you know this: God loves you and has an awesome plan for your life. It really *is* a big deal to him because he really cares about you. His plan is better than anything you could come up with for yourself. God cares about you and your life, including your love life because he wants it to be a living example of how he feels about you. That's why he wants you to be pure.

Let me close with a warning. If something you have read in this book has caused you to make a decision to follow God's plan for your life, let me give you a few hints.

1. You need to get started right away.

Don't approach it like a diet—"Yeah, I'm going to start doing that . . . next month . . . next year . . . some day." Whenever God speaks and reveals his plan, he always wants you to begin right away.

2. Your relationship with God is the most important thing.

Even though we've talked a lot about the physical war raging in your body and in this world, what is most at stake is your soul and your relationship with God. Ephesians 6:12 reminds us that our battle is against spiritual forces, even though it is fought on a physical plane.

Final Thoughts

come after you full force.

3. Anytime you decide to go deeper in your relationship with God, Satan gets pretty hacked off and will come after you full force.

You need to expect to get hit with some pretty tough resistance, especially in this area of dating, love, marriage, sex and purity. Expect temptation. Expect hard times. Expect tough decisions. Expect an all-out assault by Satan. Don't be caught off guard. He hates it when you give your life to God. Paul urges us to, "Put on the full armor of God so that you can take your stand against the devil's schemes" (Ephesians 6:11). Be strong. Be prepared. Pray every day. Spend time in God's Word. Seek out godly teaching. Guard your walk. Make good decisions. Be accountable. Choose God: his way works.

I want to say it one more time. God loves you and has a great plan for your life, especially your love life—a plan designed to protect you and provide for you, a plan modeled after his own unconditional, agapé love for you, a perfect plan to make you both happy . . . and holy. Follow that plan. The results are out of this world.

Notes

Chapter 2

[1]Jim Thornton, "USA Weekend's 10th Annual Health Report: Getting Inside Your Head," *USA WEEKEND* (January 1-3, 1999), p. 8.

[2]Ibid., p. 9.

Chapter 3

[1]"What the World's Teenagers Are Saying," *U.S. News & World Report* (June 30, 1986), p. 68.

[2]Henshaw, S., "Unintended Pregnancy in the United States," *Family Planning Perspectives* (1998), volume 30, pp. 24-29.

[3]Dorgan, C.A., *Statistical Record of Health & Medicine*, (NY: Gale Research, 1995), Table 48, pp. 315, 316.

[4]*HIV/AIDS Surveillance Report #7*, 1995, Atlanta, GA: U.S. Department of Health and Human Services, Centers for Disease Control.

[5]Henshaw, S., *U.S. Teenage Pregnancy Statistics*, (New York, NY: The Alan Guttmacher Institute, August 15, 1997).

[6]Henshaw, S., "Unintended Pregnancy in the United States," *Family Planning Perspectives* (1998), volume 30, pp. 24-29.